PIAZZA SAN

IAIN FENLON has a chair in the history of music at Cambridge where he is a Fellow of King's College. He has taught widely in Europe and the United States.

ALSO BY IAIN FENLON

The Ceremonial City: History, Memory and Myth in Renaissance Venice

Music and Culture in Late Renaissance Italy

WONDERS OF THE WORLD

....

PIAZZA SAN MARCO

IAIN FENLON

PROFILE BOOKS

This paperback edition published in 2010

First published in Great Britain in 2009 by
Profile Books Ltd
3A Exmouth House
Pine Street
Exmouth Market
London ECIR OJH
www.profilebooks.com

1 3 5 7 9 10 8 6 4 2

Typeset in Caslon by MacGuru Ltd
info@macguru.org.uk
Designed by Peter Campbell
Printed and bound in Great Britain by
CPI Bookmarque, Croydon, Surrey

A CIP catalogue record for this book is available from the British Library.

ISBN 978 1 86197 885 1
eISBN 978 1 84765 197 6

Mixed Sources
Product group from well-managed
forests and other controlled sources
www.fsc.org Cert no. TT-COC-002227
© 1996 Forest Stewardship Council
FSC

CONTENTS

For Maria-José

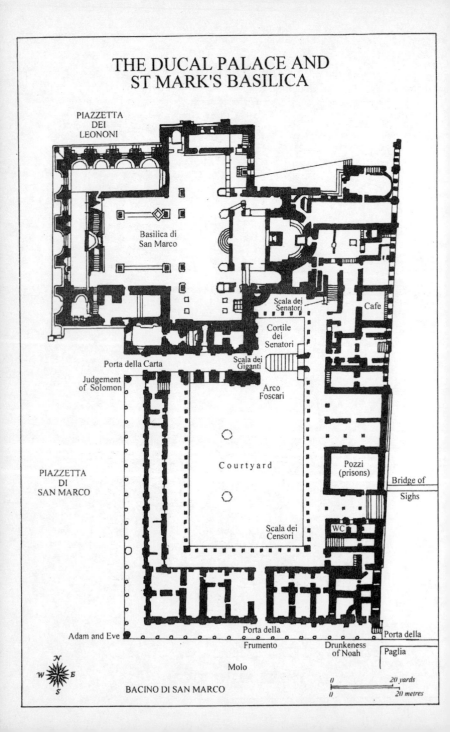

THE DUCAL PALACE AND ST MARK'S BASILICA

PIAZZETTA DEI LEONONI

Basilica di San Marco

Scala dei Senatori

Cafe

Cortile dei Senatori

Porta della Carta

Scala dei Giganti

Judgement of Solomon

Arco Foscari

Courtyard

PIAZZETTA DI SAN MARCO

Pozzi (prisons)

Bridge of

Sighs

Scala dei Censori

WC

Adam and Eve

Porta della Frumento

Drunkeness of Noah

Porta della

Paglia

Molo

N W E S

BACINO DI SAN MARCO

0   20 yards

0   20 metres

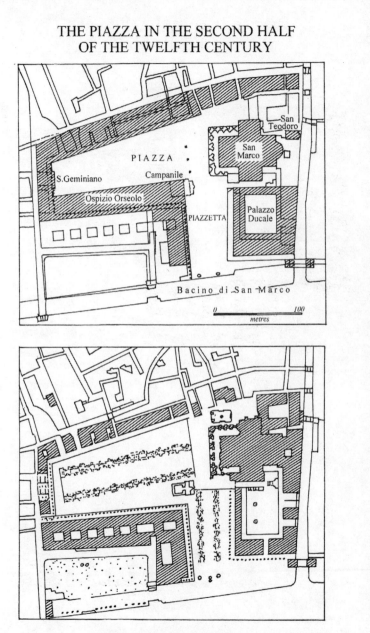

THE PIAZZA IN THE SECOND HALF
OF THE TWELFTH CENTURY

San Teodoro

San Marco

PIAZZA

S.Geminiano   Campanile

Ospizio Orseolo

Palazzo
Ducale

PIAZZETTA

Bacino di San Marco

0   100
metres

THE ST MARK'S AREA

CHRONOLOGY

775   Establishment of the episcopal see of Olivolo.

809   Pepin, son of the Emperor Charlemagne, unsuccessfully lays siege to Venice.

829   Construction of the first church of San Marco.

1063   Building of the current Basilica, consecrated in 1094, begins.

1084   Bull of Alexius Comnenus. Venice becomes an independent state.

1177   The Alexandrine Donation. Pope Alexander III presents the *trionfi* to Doge Sebastiano Venier in acknowledgement of his role in securing peace between the Pope and Emperor Federico Barbarossa.

1204   Fall of Constantinople during the Fourth Crusade. Crete becomes a Venetian colony.

1310   Failed coup of disaffected patricians.

1354   Execution of Doge Marino Falier.

1378–81   War of Chioggia. Venice is confronted by a coalition led by Genoa, its principal maritime rival.

1489   Cyprus ceded to Venice by Caterina Cornaro.

1498–1503 War against the Turks.

1508–17   War of the League of Cambrai. Venetian territory invaded by France and the Empire. Venetian forces defeated at the battle of Agnadello (1509).

INTRODUCTION

Thank God I am here! It is the Paradise of Cities.

John Ruskin, Diaries

The Piazza San Marco is the most famous and most instantly recognisable townscape in the West, if not the world. Artists have painted it, travellers have described it, poets have grown lyrical over it and architectural historians have established its evolution from a medieval field ringed by buildings to the heroic space that we know today. Although there are few books devoted exclusively to the square and its history, there are many which touch upon it in some way or other. What follows is different from most of the existing literature in that it attempts to consider the Piazza as a coherent whole, a vibrant and constantly changing public space that is related both dynamically and organically to the buildings which frame it. In this important sense the Ducal Palace, the Basilica, the Campanile (bell tower) and the other buildings with which we are so familiar not so much frame the square but are situated within it.

Understanding the Piazza in all its dimensions, social and anthropological as well as historical and architectural, is inevitably compromised if this ensemble is divided (as is the wont of most histories and guidebooks) into a series of individual structures, each 'marvellous' in its own right but also functionally separate. By relating the buildings both to each other and to the space of which they form a part, a different narrative emerges in which the square evolves as the cultural and political centre of Venice itself, the ultimate Piazza located at the centre of a once-great empire. A particular feature of this story, conceived as a sequence of narrative moments, is to put back the sound – whether the shouts of market traders or the singing of the choir of the Basilica – into the square, to bring it back to life as the focal point of the life of the city and its inhabitants. Considered as the site of everyday activities as well as a theatrical arena for the staging of the great civic and religious ceremonies of the Republic, the Piazza takes on a richer set of meanings beyond those of an inanimate, frozen architectural ensemble.

The starting point is the patron saint of Venice, Saint Mark the Evangelist. At its eastern end, the square is dominated by the Basilica dedicated to him, begun in 1063 and finally consecrated thirty years later. Embellishment with marble and mosaics, both internally and externally, continued long after this date, famously so in the case of the façade, which in its current over-restored condition is substantially a nineteenth-century creation. Many details of the external decoration, including sculptured panels, columns of marble and porphyry, and figured reliefs, came from the shiploads of loot shipped to Venice during the Fourth Crusade of 1199–1204. Most spectacular of all are the famous four bronze horses (now replaced by copies) displayed on eight short columns of white marble and four of porphyry, raised triumphantly on the loggia above the central portal of the Basilica, dramatically set against the dark central window. This prominent placing was the result of a political decision designed to emphasise not merely their beauty, but also their status as quite exceptional spoils of war, symbols of Venice's newly formulated imperial mission and of its recent status as a major commercial power at the beginning of the thirteenth century.

This had been largely achieved through contact with Byzantium – the Eastern Roman Empire – whose capital, Constantinople, was the hub of a vast intercontinental trading network. Situated within a frontier province of the Byzantine Empire, Venice was supremely placed to develop trade with the East, and as early as the ninth century merchants from the lagoon around Venice had begun to tap the rich resources of Alexandria. Economics apart, Venice was also linked to Constantinople in a political sense, since its tribunes (and later doge) were considered to be officers of the Empire. With the gradual collapse of Byzantine power in the upper Adriatic – a process whose origins have been traced to the eighth century – Venice emerged as the dominating presence in the area, a self-governing commune (*commune veneciarum*) structured along republican lines.

The critical moment came in 1204, when the Western crusade which had been originally directed against Muslim Egypt was diverted to Constantinople; the city was captured and the Empire overthrown. Together with the French, the Venetians were the main protagonists (and so the principal beneficiaries) of this military initiative. From both the internal and external appearance of the Basilica, which is modelled on the church of the Holy Apostles in Constantinople, to the ceremonies surrounding the doge, the impact of Venice's historic links to Byzantium was and is still to be seen everywhere in the Piazza, whose basic layout as a ceremonial forecourt for civic and devotional ritual, played out against the backdrop of San Marco and enclosed by a proscenium of surrounding buildings, owes more to Constantinople than to Rome.

Housing Mark's remains was the main purpose of the Basilica, but its proximity to the Palazzo Ducale also gave it a distinct civic significance even in this, the earliest phase of the transformation of San Marco from private chapel to state church. During the centuries which followed, the bonds which tied San Marco to both doge and state were strengthened through the evolution of a calendrical sequence of liturgical and civic rituals. These were enacted mostly in the Basilica, the Piazza and the Piazzetta, which for these purposes constituted a unified ceremonial area, and from where they could be processionally transported elsewhere in the city. From the very beginning of their existence, the Basilica and the ceremonial spaces which surrounded it were seen as the heart of the devotional and political geography of Venice, the centre of an intricate web of religious and civic conceptions, which were celebrated in the elaborate and spectacular processions which were such a prominent feature of the official life of the square. Witnessed by travellers, and distributed to a wider world through engravings and printed descriptions, these ritual dramas, which by the early modern period took place on some forty occasions during the year, involved the highest officers of Church and state, hierarchically arranged around the central figure of the doge.

The dogeship of Venice is without parallel in the western tradition. Although the occupant of the office was elected, he was invested with a semi-sacral authority reminiscent of medieval kingship, an aspect of the dogeship that is reflected in his participation in liturgical ritual. Surrounded by elaborate ceremonial during his lifetime, some of it clearly indebted to precedents established by the Byzantine emperors and much of it enacted in the public spaces of the Basilica and the Piazza, the doge was returned upon death to the status of ordinary citizen. Except for a few very early examples, the doges were buried not in San Marco but in their parish church, or in one of the great mendicant churches of the city. This was just one of the ways in which the Venetians, acutely conscious of the ever-present risk of dynastic control, took steps to preserve the democratic nature of the dogeship.

While in theory the doge was elected, usually late in life, from the entire patrician class, in practice he was more likely to be chosen from one of a comparatively small number of wealthy families who were rich enough to support the extravagant lifestyle that went with the post. Accommodation between the more powerful families was achieved through negotiation, powerbroking arrangements secured between members of the group of the most wealthy clans, who operated the system to their collective, mutual benefit. In the chronological list of doges from the seventh century until the arrival of Napoleon's troops in 1797 (see Appendix 1, pp. 178–82), a small number of names occur with great regularity: Particiaco, Candiano and Orseolo in the earlier centuries; Gradenigo, Contarini, Morosini and Grimani in the later ones. Between 1450 and 1620, members of the Barbarigo, Grimani, Loredan and Venier families each held the office twice, while the Donà, Mocenigo and Priuli families did so three times. Over the centuries steps were taken to curtail the power of the doge. So much so that, in the opinion of many commentators, by the middle of the sixteenth century he had become a largely ceremonial figurehead devoid of any real political power. Donato Giannotti (1492–1573), a Florentine by birth, who together with Gasparo Contarini (1483–1542) was one of the two most influential constitutional theorists of the period, wrote that

> *the insignia of the Venetian empire are invested in the person of the doge, since in the Republic only he has the appearance of a lord. But though he alone possesses such dignity, he is not given complete power in anything, since not only is he unable to make decisions however insignificant, but also he cannot do anything without his councillors.*

Contarini, who was Venetian and in consequence less influenced by Florentine republicanism inspired by Machiavellian opposition to the Medici, claimed something very similar. It is noticeable that, as the power of the doge declined, the ceremonies and rituals that surrounded him became both more elaborate and more frequent.

In the absence of classical Roman origins, the legends that surrounded Saint Mark's relation to Venice became the cornerstone of the foundation myth of the state itself. During the second half of the eleventh century, while the church was being built, the Piazza San Marco began to take on a more formal appearance, and 100 years later the creation of a new civic Piazza was initiated by the Venetian government to order and embellish what had evolved as the main politico-ecclesiastical centre of the city. At this stage the main features of the area were the Basilica, the Palazzo Ducale and the Campanile, which served the practical function of summoning the members of the Great Council to business, announcing the death of the doge and the election of his successor, and articulating other ritual and official moments in the life of the Republic. Much altered over the centuries, the Campanile has become almost a symbol for Venice itself; as such it has been much copied, not only in Venice and on the *terraferma* (the mainland territories of the Republic), but as far away as the Strip at Las Vegas where, together with facsimiles of the Rialto Bridge, the Ca D'Oro and the Palazzo Ducale, it forms part of a new hotel complex which 're-creates the romance, Old-World charm and festival-like atmosphere of Old Venice'.

The next major change to the appearance of Saint Mark's Square took place in the sixteenth century following the appointment of Jacopo Sansovino (1486–1570) as state architect. This placed Sansovino under the patronage of the wealthiest sponsors of new building work anywhere in the city, at a time when the political will to remodel the Piazza and its surrounding buildings was strong; the consequence was an ambitious *renovatio urbis*, inaugurated during the dogeship of Andrea Gritti (1455–1538), and carried out with his active encouragement. As it unfolded, Sansovino's task was to inaugurate the first phase of a grandiose plan to line the three landlocked sides of the Piazza and the Piazzetta together with the eastern end of the Molo (the quayside at the entrance to the Grand Canal) with new structures in the classical style. By the time of his death, the Loggetta at the foot of the Campanile, the library facing the Palazzo Ducale and the Mint had all been completed. Sansovino's overall conception has been seen not only as a conscious attempt to evolve, in architectural terms, the 'Myth of Venice' through the use of a distinctive classicising language, but also as a courageous reinterpretation, on a monumental scale, of the typology of the ancient Roman forum as described by Marcus Vitruvius Pollio (*c.* 80 BCE – *c.* 15 BCE). Finished in the seventeenth century, Sansovino's scheme has survived intact except for its western flank, demolished in the early nineteenth century to create a suitably imperial setting in the neoclassical style for Venice's new master, Napoleon, who had taken over the city in 1797. At the same time, some of Venice's treasures were removed, among them the four horses, which were shipped to Paris where they duly spawned their own progeny in the gardens of the Tuileries.

In common with the Roman forum as described by Vitruvius, Saint Mark's Square was not only used for public meetings and popular celebrations (particularly during the carnival season which preceded Lent), but was also a market place, where fish and meat were sold among other things. This had been true since the beginning of its history. Taverns operated in the square, pilgrims gathered to change money and arrange to travel to the Holy Land, charlatans and tooth-pullers plied their trades under the clocktower and bread was baked in ovens. Markets were held in the Piazza with some regularity. Once a week an official open market took place there, and the most important trade fair of the year, which was organised in conjunction with the Festa del Sensa (a ritual celebration of the Feast of the Ascension), involved the construction of temporary shopping arcades around the square. Some of these activities can still be seen in the paintings of Canaletto (1697–1768), a gentle reminder that, before Napoleon's arrival, the square was closer in spirit and function to an Arab souk than to the forecourt at Versailles. Yet while the everyday life of the square was not always consonant with the heroic solemnity of Jacopo Sansovino's architecture, it was rarely as moribund as the images of official ceremonies and processions suggest. News-sheets and popular prints were hawked in the Piazza by itinerant vendors around the Basilica, and strolling players – the forebears of today's performers of Viennese salon music – stood on benches and improvised staging to entertain the crowds. On occasion the square became the site of more sombre rituals when, under the watchful gaze of the figure of Justice on the façade of the Ducal Palace, criminals were executed between the two columns in the Piazzetta.

The appearance of Piazza San Marco, as it changed over the centuries, is intimately connected to the successive political concerns of the Venetians, to the shifting emphases of official policy, and to the changing fortunes of the Republic. In this sense both the square itself and the activities that took place within it can be seen as a barometer of Venetian history and identity over a thousand-year period. But to give it life it is necessary to recreate not only the rituals of the past but also the activities of the present, from the coronation of the doge to the celebrated Pink Floyd concert of 1989, with much in between. Here the intention is to imaginatively recreate and in some sense restore the vitality of the square, to put back sound, colour and motion into the heart of the city, an iconic space which the writings of traditional historians have often left dead and silent.

I

....

MYTHS AND ORIGINS

A few in fear
Flying away from him, whose boast it was
That the grass grew not where his horse had trod,
Gave birth to Venice. Like the water-fowl,
They built their nests above the ocean waves;
And where the sands were shifting, as the wind
Blew from the north or south – where they that came
Had to make sure the ground they stood upon
Rose, like an exhalation from the deep,
A vast metropolis, with glistening spires,
With theatres, basilicas adorned;
A scene of light and glory, a dominion,
That has endured the longest among men.

Samuel Rogers, *Italy*

Unlike so many Italian towns and cities, Venice cannot claim Roman origins. Until the fifth century CE most of the lagoon on which it lies was a vast uninhabited malarial swamp, a remote, dangerous, mysterious and even secret place, largely inhabited by wildfowl nesting among the reeds, and by the occasional transients who braved the uncertain tides, the treacherous sandbanks and the inhospitable climate to fish

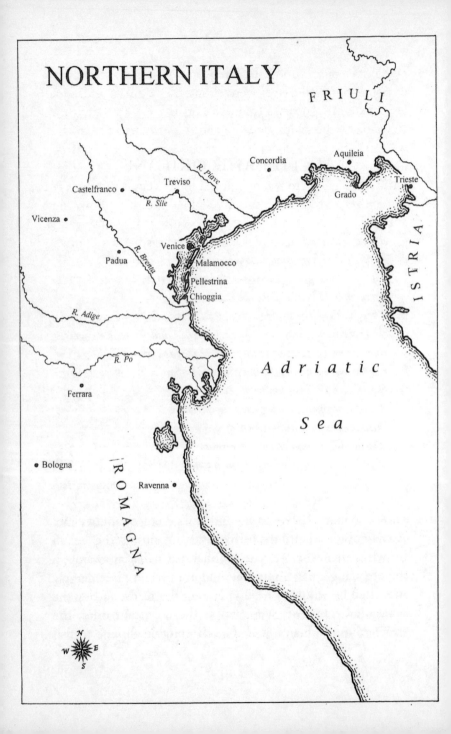

and gather salt. During the late Roman Empire the centres of population and power were elsewhere: Aquileia and, to a lesser extent, Concordia (modern Portogruaro) in the north, Ravenna to the south, and the ancient city of Padua to the west. All this changed with the arrival of the Visigoths, who, under the leadership of Alaric (*c.* 370–410), swept through Istria and Venetia to reach Aquileia in 402; eight years afterwards they famously sacked Rome. Half a century later, the even fiercer depredations of the legendary Attila the Hun (406–53), immortalised in Giuseppe Verdi's patriotic opera *Attila* (1846), brought devastation to much of north Italy. This included, once again, Aquileia, which this time was definitively and ruthlessly ransacked. Apart from a handful of buildings – notably the Basilica, whose fourth-century mosaic pavement and much of whose early structure miraculously survive – what had been the ninth largest city of the Roman Empire now lay in ruins. In the following years, as many of the towns and villages in the surrounding countryside suffered a similar fate at the hands of Attila's savage soldiery, the flow of refugees to the islands of the lagoon increased. Venice was founded as a consequence of devastation in the countryside and the flight from the mainland. It is this – a community founded on fear – that the English poet Samuel Rogers (1763–1855) so eloquently captures in his poem above, the first significant portrayal of the city as a dream-like ruin, a site of enchantment, a 'vast metropolis, with glistening spires'.

In practice, the 'exhalation from the deep' invoked by Rogers was to take centuries. In the meantime, struggling to survive in these unpromising conditions, the Venetians evolved a way of life that required both resilience and ingenuity. The German poet Johann Goethe (1749–1832), who visited the city only a few years before the end of the Republic following the French invasion in 1797, sensed these fundamental aspects of the Venetian character, shaped over the centuries by life in a dangerous and threatening environment:

> *This race did not seek refuge in these islands for fun, nor were those who joined later moved by chance; necessity taught them to find safety in the most unfavourable location. Later, however, this turned out to their greatest advantage and made them wise at a time when the whole northern world still lay in darkness; their increasing population and wealth were a logical consequence. Houses were crowded closer and closer together, sand and swamp transformed into solid pavement ... The place of street and square and promenade were taken by water. In consequence, the Venetian was bound to develop into a new kind of creature, and that is why, too, Venice can only be compared to itself.*

In 466, representatives of the various communities scattered around the Venetian archipelago gathered at Grado, six miles south of Aquileia (see map, p. 2) to establish a loose federation based on common political interests. This was to be governed by tribunes who were annually elected, and it was from this primitive assembly that the Republic of Venice gradually evolved through a slow, cumulative constitutional process. Some sense of the tenor of everyday life during the earliest phase of the lagoon settlement comes through strongly in a remarkable document, unusual for its period in being secular rather than ecclesiastical in origin, written in 523 by a Roman administrative official called Cassiodorus. Writing as the praetorian prefect of Italy to the 'maritime tribunes' of the area, in the hope of exacting a tribute of olive oil from Istria, Cassiodorus attempts to persuade the islanders that his request should be easy to meet by using seductive rhetoric:

> ... *for you live like sea birds, with your homes dispersed, like the Cyclades, across the surface of the water. The solidity of the earth on which they rest is secured only by osier and wattle; yet you do not hesitate to oppose so frail a bulwark to the wildness of the sea. Your people have one great wealth – the fish which suffices for them all. Among you there is no difference between rich and poor; your food is the same, your houses are all alike. Envy, which rules the rest of the world, is unknown to you. All your energies are spent on your salt-fields; in them indeed lies your prosperity, and your power to purchase those things which you have not. For though there may be men who have little need of gold, yet none live who desire not salt. Be diligent, therefore, to repair your boats – which, like horses, you keep tied up at the doors of your dwellings – and make haste to depart ...*

Even allowing for some exaggeration, and the ingratiating tone (these were evidently people to be cultivated, respected and wooed), an appreciation of Venetian fortitude and toughness in the face of considerable odds comes through strongly. A boat from one of the tiny settlements on the lagoon, preserved in the Natural History Museum in Venice, is a potent reminder of the mastery of the sea displayed by the first Venetians, and an oddly moving confirmation of the Venetian world conjured up by Cassiodorus.

The houses to which he refers, evidently from first-hand observation, were presumably made of wood, raised on stilts for protection, and, although no significant traces of these have been discovered, carbon-dating has established that what later became Piazza San Marco was settled in the sixth century, at about the time that Cassiodorus was writing. As late as the ninth century, when the settlement at Rivo Alto (hence Rialto) became the capital of the Venetian state, and the city began to expand, most of the buildings were still constructed of wood, with thatched roofs. Only the most important and official structures, notably the church of San Marco (founded as the private chapel of the doge; the first holder of the post was elected at the end of the eleventh century) and the Palazzo Ducale (the Doge's Palace), were built of brick and stone. By this time, in the aftermath of the peace of 811 between Emperor Charlemagne and the Byzantine Empire, Rome's successor in the East, Venice had been designated as a province of Byzantium. Construction of the first church of San Marco, designed to house the body of Saint Mark the Evangelist, which had been brought to Venice in 828, was begun shortly afterwards on the instructions of Doge Giustiniano Particiaco. The site chosen was close to the Palace, which had been created out of the ancient castle by Particiaco's immediate predecessor. This was not only a matter of administrative convenience; from the very start of the Venetian state, founded on possession of Saint Mark's body and its presence at the physical and spiritual heart of the city, temporal and religious authority were both practically and symbolically linked.

Of this original church almost nothing can be seen. Although archaeologists differ on how exactly it might have looked, it seems likely that the original ninth-century structure followed the simple form of a Greek cross, with an apse at the eastern end and a central dome over the crossing. It was substantially built of brick (as is the present building), with stone and marble being used only for columns and decorative finishes. All this was probably roofed in wood. The line of its façade is buried under the present church, coinciding with the wall between its nave and its atrium. Stone from various sources, including Roman monuments on the mainland, was used in its construction. Beyond this little can be said. Damaged in the fire that ravaged Venice during the revolt against Doge Pietro IV Candiano in 976, this first church was reconstructed by his successors. This second church lasted less than a century before it too was replaced by the present building, begun in 1063 during the dogeship of Domenico Contarini, but not consecrated until some thirty years later.

In the absence of clear Roman roots for their city, the Venetians developed a number of different legends to explain its origins. Alaric's invasion provided the raw material for one of them, according to which Venice was established by a contingent of young aristocratic refugees from nearby Padua. The main source for this piece of mythology, a chronicle written by the fourteenth-century Paduan physician Jacopo Dondi (and therefore susceptible to local aggrandisement), provides the additional, if implausible, detail that this took place at noon on 25 March 421, thus ingeniously conflating the precise moment of the city's foundation with the beginning of the Venetian year on the feast of the Annunciation. The accuracy of the story must be seriously doubted. There is no record of sustained Paduan colonisation of the lagoon during the fifth century, and the date itself is far too early for any such initiative to have been made by its inhabitants, dispersed in flight from the barbarian invasions which took place at precisely the same time. Despite its implausibility, the date of 25 March 421 echoes down the centuries in all the major works of official Venetian history. It is still there in the first and most influential guidebook to the city and its monuments, Francesco Sansovino's *Venetia città nobilissima*, published in 1581 and reprinted twice within the next hundred years. Born in 1521 in Rome, the son of the architect Jacopo Sansovino whose re-modelling of the Piazza San Marco gave it so much of its present-day appearance, Francesco was a versatile scholar, writer and publisher. *Venetia città nobilissima* is still an invaluable source of information about the city and its early history.

Another account of the origins of Venice was offered in the late fifteenth century by the Venetian historian Marcantonio Sabellico (1436–1506), who in 1485 presented the government with his *History of Venice*, written in thirty-three books and modelled on Livy's history of ancient Rome. According to this, the first settlers of the lagoon had come not from mainland Italy but from Gaul, which gave them greater status in contemporary eyes. An alternative theory, equally without historical evidence, claims that the first inhabitants of Venice were Trojan refugees who had fetched up in Italy after the destruction of their city by the Greeks, centuries before Christ. The state official Martin da Canal, in his chronicle *Les estoires de Venise*, written in the late thirteenth century, was one of the first writers to make the claim that a number of cities in the Upper Adriatic, including both Aquileia and Venice, had been founded in this way; in effect this is an extension of the claim made in passing in the *Aeneid* that Padua, like Rome, was a Trojan foundation. Both these fantasy legends are ingeniously united in another text, Bernardo Giustiniani's *De origine urbis Venetiarum*, published in 1493, just eight years after Sabellico's book came off the presses. While the first explanation encouraged Venetian friendship with the French, the Trojan theory introduced the cherished idea of Venetian *libertas*, or freedom from outside control, one of the central tenets of the 'Myth of Venice', as well as injecting the noble blood of heroic warriors into Venetian veins. Despite Giustiniani's reputation as the first authoritative humanist scholar of Venice, it was the Trojan theory that found most favour with later writers.

Some time after finishing his account of the origins of Venice, Giustiniani composed three short works dealing with the life of Saint Mark. He explains the relationship between these and his earlier history:

> When I had determined to write about the origin of the city of Venice, I remember that I mentioned in the beginning of the work that nothing had happened in the founding of Venice which was usual in the establishment of other cities; neither walls, nor gates, nor even fortresses were constructed. Then it occurred to me that a few years after the transference of the Dogeship, the most holy Mark, the Evangelist, was carried off by Venetian merchants from the city of Alexandria, where he had lain for nearly eight hundred years, and he was brought to Venice. Therefore I considered it neither irrelevant to our subject nor beside the point to add also this to those matters which I have so far set forth. I decided to record in what way he, almost as a founder, and certainly as a noble protector, came to this new city, by whose vigilance and patronage it was finally rendered unconquerable and impregnable.

As Giustiniani clearly realised, the Venetians' appropriation of Mark, which secured a holy protector of the first rank, was a political act of fundamental importance. In effect, it laid the foundations of the state. In addition, while clearly separating the political and religious strands in his account of the foundation of Venice, Giustiniani treats much of the mythology surrounding Mark as historical truth. In the second work of his trilogy dealing with the Evangelist, he returns to the story of what came to be known as the *translatio*, the transferral of the Evangelist's body from Alexandria in 828, and to its sequel, the construction of the Basilica. In the final essay, *On the Place of Burial*, the evidence is amassed for the presence of the saint's remains inside the building. Giustiniani's text is prefaced with a short biography of Mark which isolates the most significant moments in his life: the composition of a gospel; his foundation of the Church in Aquileia and Alexandria; his invention of the monastic life; and finally his martyrdom. It was this heroic trajectory which was transmitted to Venice itself, the resting place of his relics. There it formed the cornerstone of the city's civic greatness, its unbroken traditions of liberty and its sacred laws, all of which were embodied in evolving rituals of Church and state which connected the changing history of the Republic, from its foundation onwards, to the realities of evolving ceremonial. Nowhere was this more powerfully evoked than in Piazza San Marco and its surrounding buildings, which served both as the focal points of these rituals, and as the ultimate expression of the central tenets of Venetian political theology, which defined a sense of identity for the Republic and its citizens. It is with Mark that this mythology, religious before it became political, really starts.

This point is neatly underlined by the opening chapter

of fourteenth-century Doge Andrea Dandolo's chronicle – perhaps the most important of all the early accounts of the origins of Venice – which starts with Saint Mark's visit to Aquileia on the orders of Saint Peter. Critically, this places Mark in the Upper Adriatic in the first years of Christianity. It should be said immediately that Dandolo's opening gambit is without any kind of historical evidence, either literary or archaeological. There are no traces of the cult of Mark in the region during the early Christian period, as might be expected if such a visit had actually taken place. None the less, it was as a result of the traditional story that Aquileia had been established by Saint Mark in person that its metropolitan archbishop came to occupy a position in the Italian ecclesiastical hierarchy second only to the pope. In all probability, the legend of Saint Mark's time in Aquileia is a piece of carefully crafted mythology, invented to meet political and ecclesiastical circumstances in the aftermath of the schism of 606, when the original patriarchate of Aquileia was divided into two. The first of these remained under Aquileian control, while the second, which included Istria and the islands of the lagoon that were later to become Venice itself, came under the jurisdiction of Grado. Significantly, it was the patriarch of Grado who possessed the ancient episcopal throne which, according to legend, Mark himself had once occupied. Such matters lay at the heart of frequent jurisdictional disputes between Venice and Aquileia in the early middle ages. In this context, the myth of Mark's visit is highly characteristic of a whole complex of stories relating to him, an inventive mixture of reality and legend which was developed in response to political difficulties during the Carolingian period. The texts which transmit these stories, the buildings which celebrate them, the mosaics, fresco cycles and altar-pieces which depict them, and the liturgies and ritual objects which articulate them, are not only things of beauty and historical fascination in themselves, but are also evidence of a sequence of politically constructed conflations of civic and religious ideas which provided the basis for local identities. The whole complex of stories about Mark, and the political realities of struggle, claim and counter-claim against which they are played out, is in consequence also central to our understanding of the origins, nature and development of the Piazza San Marco itself.

The earliest account of Mark's visit to Aquileia, written by Paul the Deacon in the eighth century, gives an abbreviated version of Mark's mission to the area, but importantly it also adds the detail of Mark's choice of Hermagoras as his disciple and successor. According to Paul, the two then travelled together to Rome, where Hermagoras was consecrated as the first bishop of Aquileia by Saint Peter himself. This too is an invention; presumably the story was devised in order to strengthen the concept of apostolic succession by giving it papal approval. As a mythological move this is typical of the way that the legends surrounding Mark were constantly adapted for political purposes. Equally characteristic of the genre is that, once this fresh episode had been attached to the original legend, it remained firmly in place. In this way, the Evangelist's apostolic journey to Aquileia constitutes in turn the first phase of a whole sequence of legends, and becomes the interpretational lever for the most powerful of all of them, the story of the *translatio*.

The essential features of this narrative centre on the adventures of a couple of merchants, Tribunus and Rusticus, from two islands in the lagoon, both of which were important administrative and ecclesiastical centres before Venice itself was established. The merchants' ship, together with nine others, is driven off course to Alexandria, an act of fate used to justify their trade with the Saracens, which was otherwise restricted. Second in size and importance of all the cities of the Roman Empire, Alexandria was home to the largest Jewish community of the ancient world. According to tradition, Christianity was brought to the city by Mark, who was himself a Jew and had earlier worked in Rome with Saint Paul. Hearing of the caliph of Alexandria's plans to desecrate Mark's tomb, the two merchants resolve to steal the body and escort it to Venice. In order to do this, it is necessary for them to persuade the two Greek custodians of the tomb to collaborate. Seizing on the claim that Mark had evangelised Aquileia and the surrounding area before arriving in Alexandria, Tribunus and Rusticus argue that it is appropriate that his body should be returned to the lagoon where it belongs. There it would be safe from Arab marauders. Faced with these arguments, the custodians relent and agree to the scheme. The plan is nearly discovered when the fragrance given off by the relics arouses suspicion, but once this danger has passed the conspirators place Mark's remains in a basket and cover them with pork. The smell of the forbidden meat repels the Muslim customs officers who take to their heels in disgust. Mark's body is then safely smuggled on board. After a troublefree voyage, the crew is roused from sleep by Mark himself, whose warning that they are close to shore averts disaster.

This story is the first of a sequence of miracles required by contemporary hagiography for the authentication of relics. A second soon follows when, having landed on the Istrian coast, the crew successfully repels an infestation of devils. Once the galley arrives in Venice it is greeted not, as had been feared, by official reprimands, but by the gratitude of Bishop Ursus of Olivolo-Castello (the bishop of the city) and his clergy, who immediately accompany the relics in a solemn procession to the Doge's Palace. Once the body is inside the palace, the cycle of miracles is completed. The doge, Giustiniano Parteciaco, vows to build a new church to house the relics, but dies before his promise can be executed. It is carried out by his successor.

Whether any of the events in this sequence actually happened is not the issue, though the balance of opinion is surely on the side of doubt. But as an indicator of Venetian political concerns, the text of the *translatio* is very revealing. In choosing Mark as their principal patron, the Venetians effectively outbid Aquileia and its Carolingian supporters in the international game of acquiring prestigious relics. Thereafter Venice was in a quite different category from Aquileia, which was merely associated with Mark through the spurious story of his brief time in the area. Possession was all. The presence of Mark's relics effectively provided the foundation stone of the Venetian state, based on a precise configuration of civic and religious conceptions. As such the story was to be endlessly repeated, celebrated, elaborated and illustrated over the centuries.

In order to adopt Mark, the Venetians relegated their existing patron saint, the Greek warrior Theodore of Heraclea, to secondary status. In Mark, not only a 'Roman' saint in the sense that he lived in Rome with Saints Peter and Paul but also an evangelist who wrote his gospel there, they found a fitting agent for a new collective identity as Venice entered a final phase of emancipation from Byzantine sovereignty and moved towards independence; the substitution of Mark for Theodore, an Eastern saint, also implicitly recognised the waning power of Byzantium itself. Nevertheless, Theodore continued to be an important figure in the Venetian panoply of saints, and a significant presence in the Venetian collective consciousness as one of the principal defenders of the city and its citizens. This role is symbolised by the positioning of his statue, paired with that of the Winged Lion of Saint Mark, on one of the two columns at the entrance to the Piazzetta San Marco, which leads into the main Piazza from the lagoon. This is a highly significant position, close to both the Basilica and the Ducal Palace, the symbols of ecclesiastical and political power, and at the formal entrance to the Piazza. Passing between the columns, processions escorting important visitors to the Basilica and the Doge's Palace were overseen by two holy guardians, one Byzantine, the other Roman. In raising these two sculptures in the late twelfth century, the Venetians were confirming both in their dual capacity as Christian symbols and civic icons. This counterpoint of Eastern and Western saints, Theodore and Mark, Byzantium and Rome, is typical of twelfth-century Venetian culture, with its constant appeals to imperial models in the search for a rhetoric thought to be suitable for its increasingly important status. Mark, incessantly invoked through the image of the winged lion, may have replaced Theodore as the principal patron saint of the Republic, but Theodore was never entirely forgotten. His relevance was still recognised at the end of the fifteenth century by Marin Sanudo (1466–1536), author of an unusually detailed and extensive diary in which he meticulously chronicles everyday life and important events during his lifetime. As late as 1552 the minor confraternity (*Scuola piccola*) which bore Theodore's name was elevated to the status of a *Scuola grande*. Since there were only six such charitable bodies in the city, this was a clear sign of his position in the civic and religious life of Venice.

The story of the *translatio* of Saint Mark's body was more than a just legend. In a world in which Roman origins lent a city status and defined its identity, Venice had previously been at a disadvantage. The acquisition of Mark solved the problem by providing the ideological underpinning of both Church and state. By bringing Mark's relics to their city, the Venetian ruling class aggressively pursued the objective of defining a new sacral geography. In its agglomeration of political and ecclesiastical ideologies for use in the construction of a collective memory, the *translatio* is characteristic of an entire medieval genre that served both devotional and political purposes. In Venice, the four major Venetian feast days associated with Mark were not only celebrations of the life of the Evangelist, but also allegories for constitutional and military events.

Regardless of its weak historical foundations, the *translatio* fulfilled its political purpose brilliantly. By simultaneously achieving Venetian independence from both Byzantium and Aquileia, it secured Parteciaco's objective of uniting Venetian settlements and towns around a religious centre directly under the control of the doge. Beginning with Martin da Canal, the legend of the *translatio* became the basis for the many retellings of the legend in the Venetian chronicle tradition, and from there it found its way into the popular printed histories that spread the legend to a wider world in the age of print. From the late middle ages onwards, the main outlines of the story provided medieval and Renaissance artists from Venice and the surrounding area with a rich fund of material.

Canal's *Les estoires de Venise* (1275) is also the earliest written source for an important modification to the foundation narrative, elaborated around the middle of the thirteenth century, during a period of prolific growth in state-controlled myth-making about the city and its origins. The new episode, which is recounted in its fullest form in Dandolo's chronicle, concerns the saint's journey to Rome with Hermagoras. Surprised by a sudden storm in the lagoon, Mark rows their boat to a small island, which in later accounts is identified not only as the island of Rialto, but even more precisely as the place where the church of San Marco was later to be built. The saint falls asleep, and in a dream hears the voice of an angel announcing that this is to be his final resting place: '*Pax tibi, Marce, Evangelista meus. Hic requiescat corpus tuum*'; 'Peace to you, Mark, my Evangelist. On this spot shall your body rest.' This promise to Mark, made while he was still alive, that Venice would be his ultimate resting place, is known as the *praedestinatio*. A prefiguration of the *translatio*, which it made inevitable, the *praedestinatio* provided yet further ammunition for the potent idea of Venice as the ultimate privileged and divinely protected Christian republic. Together with the ceremony of the 'Marriage to the Sea' introduced about the same time, in which the doge is taken in a ceremonial barge (*bucintoro*) to the mouth of the lagoon and throws a gold ring into the waters, the *praedestinatio* is yet further evidence of the thirteenth-century bout of Venetian self-confidence which followed the conquest of Constantinople in 1204. In practical terms it allowed both the transferral of Mark's relics and the construction of a temple to house them to be seen as divinely ordained, and as such sanctioned by the highest authority. In addition, the episode provided the saint's bones with a prehistory that both anticipated and justified the *translatio* itself. It is no accident that this came about at the same time that Venice became genuinely independent. Between the ninth and the twelfth centuries it, together with Genoa, Pisa and Amalfi, had evolved into a 'maritime republic'. Now, with the Byzantine Empire virtually exhausted, the strategic position of Venice at the head of the Adriatic made its naval and commercial strength almost invincible. Quite simply, it had grown into the most powerful city state in the world.

The story of Mark's visit to the lagoon became a standard part of theological literature. Jacobus de Voraigne's popular *Golden Legend* (1275), for example, a compilation of anecdotal biographies of the saints that remained in vogue well into the era of the printed book, claimed that Mark's body 'was returned to Italy so that the land where it had been given him to write his gospel won the privilege of possessing his sacred remains'. More immediately, for most citizens of the Republic the legend of Mark's visit provided the text for that most familiar image of the Venetian state, and of the saint whose relics gave it its meaning: the Winged Lion of Saint Mark. He came in various versions. The most commonly encountered presents the lion rampant, moving forward with determination on all four paws. Another familiar type shows just the head, described as 'a *molecche*' by the Venetians, since the image resembled the soft-shell crabs (*molecche*), now a great delicacy, that are fished out of the lagoon during a brief season in early autumn. Inscribed on coins, woven in silk thread on the ceremonial banners carried at the head of the *andata* or ducal procession, and incised on the innumerable stone tablets that proclaimed the authority of the Serenissima from the towns and cities of the mainland and the Venetian colonies abroad, the Evangelist's emblem represented the state itself and all that it stood for. So potent was the image of the Winged Lion that one of the first acts of the French authorities after the fall of the Republic in 1797 was to remove it from its column in the Piazzetta and ship it off to Paris.

....

IMPERIAL VISIONS

'Such, then, was that first and fairest Venice which rose out of the barrenness of the lagoon, and the sorrow of her people; a city of graceful arcades and gleaming walls, veined with azure and warm with gold, and fretted with white sculpture like frost upon forest branches turned to marble.'

John Ruskin, *The Stones of Venice*

From the arrival of Mark's body in the ninth century flowed an identification with the saint as the special protector of the city which crucially determined the character of much Venetian ritual and of the spaces in which it was performed. The most immediate and dramatic consequence was the planning and construction of a building to house them, significantly enough not in Grado – then the seat of the bishop – but in Venice itself, where Mark's relics had been deposited through divine agency. Building began shortly afterwards, in accordance with the terms of Giustiniano Parteciaco's will, which specified that a church in honour of the Evangelist was to be constructed within the boundaries of the land belonging to the Benedictine convent and church of San Zaccaria, which stands in the same part of Venice but further to the east. Significantly, the construction of the church now became not only a direct consequence of the *translatio*, but also the result of an initiative made by an individual doge, brought to fruition by his younger brother Giovanni, who succeeded him in office. Henceforward, in keeping with the characteristic mixture of religious and civic elements which make up the foundation myth of Venice itself, the image of Mark was indissolubly wedded to the office of doge and to the concept of ducal authority. In 832, this first church was formally consecrated.

Housing the relics of an important saint was not merely a building project; it also brought status and authority to the site. Virtually nothing remains of this first church, but the consensus view is that its ground plan was based on that of Emperor Justinian I's church of the Holy Apostles in Constantinople, originally built in 550 but reconstructed under Justinian after its symbolic destruction by Mehmet the Conqueror. Designed on a cruciform plan, this is where the relics of Saint Andrew, the alleged founder of the patriarchate in Constantinople, were preserved. The idea of a basilica to house apostolic relics was not in itself new, the earliest Italian example being that founded by Saint Ambrose during his time in Milan in the second half of the fourth century. This had in turn provided the model for others elsewhere in Italy, including a number of sanctuaries founded in Ravenna by Justinian, who wished to make that city the centre of the Italian Church in place of Rome. In pursuing this ambitious politico-ecclesiastical objective, Justinian's possession of apostolic remains was a fundamental weapon and, in formulating their own plans, the Venetians may well have had his example in mind. Clearly they were conscious of the advantages in terms of status that comparison with these magnificent precedents would bring. From the beginning, San Marco was conceived as a grandiloquent expression of newly found standing in the world; the effect was regal, if not imperial.

The decision to construct the Basilica next to the Ducal Palace (later still the two buildings were to be physically linked) was a move of great symbolic significance. Although providing a suitable resting place for Mark's relics was the main purpose of the new building, its proximity to the Palace also gave it a distinct civic meaning. During the centuries which followed, the bonds which tied Saint Mark to both doge and state were strengthened through the evolution of a characteristically Venetian mixture of liturgical and civic rituals. These were enacted mostly in the Basilica, the Piazza and the adjoining Piazzetta, which for these purposes constituted a unified ceremonial area. From there they were also transported to other locations in the city, when the *andata*, the elaborately choreographed ducal procession, visited sites of particular historical or religious significance. Typically these were parish churches, convents and monasteries, which were often associated with major events in Venetian history, usually military or naval victories. In this way the Piazza functioned as the heart of the devotional and political geography of the city, and the heart of its ceremonial and ritual life. Taken together, the Basilica, the Ducal Palace and the spaces which surrounded them operated as the centre of an intricate web of religious and civic conceptions, celebrated in a number of distinct processional acts which involved the highest officers of Church and state.

Although architectural historians and archaeologists have been inventive in their attempts to reconstruct the first church, it is quite impossible to imagine how it actually looked except in the most general terms. The same is true for the second church, which lasted less than a century before it too was replaced by the present building. Begun during the early years of the dogeship of Domenico Contarini in the mid eleventh century, the present Basilica di San Marco was not finally consecrated until 1094. For this third church on the site it seems that the Venetians once again chose as their model the church of the Holy Apostles in Constantinople. On to its basic cruciform plan with five domes were grafted elements from both middle Byzantine architecture and Italian practice. This was not merely a matter of following an existing architectural model; the parallels between the two churches also imply ambitious political motivations. Both housed the relics of an apostle and, in selecting an imperial prototype for the ducal Basilica di San Marco, Contarini and his advisers were making a powerful statement in the continuing struggle with Aquileia for political and ecclesiastical supremacy in the Upper Adriatic. Once again, the political and the religious components of the Venetian identity, at least in its official formulation, were inextricably intertwined.

In its original finished form, San Marco did not much resemble the splendid and ornate building that we are used to today, nor even the late fifteenth-century church that forms the background of Gentile Bellini's large narrative painting of 1496 showing a *Procession in the Piazza San Marco*, one of a cycle of scenes showing miracles connected to the relic of the True Cross owned by the Scuola Grande di San Giovanni, who commissioned them to decorate their meeting hall (see illustration 1). Although most of the area occupied by the present building was originally part of the eleventh-century structure, some components were probably remains of earlier churches on the same site, while yet others received

1. Gentile Bellini's *Procession* of 1496 showing one of the six main Venetian confraternities carrying their prized relic of the True Cross around the Piazza. In the background can be seen the Basilica as it was before the extensive later restorations of the façade and its mosaics.

their present shape only in later centuries. The exterior has changed even more. Originally it was faced in brick, and most of the marble cladding, friezes and sculptures that now decorate it were added in the first half of the thirteenth century, when both the north and west atria were added (although the three central bays of the west atrium probably existed earlier). The façade cycle of mosaics, which acts as a preface to the building itself and serves as a reminder of the church's principal function as the repository of Mark's body, was executed at about the same time, though both internal and external decoration continued long after this date; some of the mosaic work was not completed until as late as the nineteenth century. Many details of the external ornamentation, including columns of marble and porphyry, figured reliefs and the celebrated four horses placed above the main portico, came from the shiploads of trophies shipped to Venice after the capture of Constantinople in 1204. The horses, imported by the Venetians, captured by the French under Napoleon, returned by the Austrians two decades later, removed to Rome for safety during two world wars, and finally installed inside the Museo della Basilica in the 1980s to minimise the effects of pollution, recur as a motif throughout Venetian history, articulating its main events. The removal of booty of all kinds, from precious building materials to reliquaries, manuscripts, chalices and icons, continued until the collapse in 1261 of the Latin Kingdom. Many of the most spectacular items in the Treasury of the Basilica arrived as a consequence.

The north side of the Basilica, overlooking the Piazzetta dei Leoncini, contains a somewhat haphazard arrangement of decorative elements, randomly selected (it would seem) for their ornamental qualities rather than for their place in any planned iconographical scheme. The balancing façade on the south side, and the area immediately surrounding it, is differently organised, being rich in triumphal motifs; these include the so-called 'Pillars of Acre', the famed porphyry tetrarchs or 'Moors' and the Pietra del Bando, all trophies from Venetian military adventures. Political correctness now frowns on their removal from their original sites, but this was hardly a contemporary perception. According to a practice that dates at least from Roman times, spoils were regarded as victor's booty, fit to be transported to a suitable place of authority where they could be displayed as symbols of conquest. Each has its own story. The Pietra del Bando, a squat stump of a porphyry column from which official decrees were read and the heads of traitors displayed, was probably removed by Lorenzo Tiepolo from Acre in 1258, where it had been used as a symbol of Genoese authority. The 'Moors', an ensemble sculpted in porphyry, thought by some scholars to represent Diocletian and three other Emperors and by others the four sons of Constantine, long suspected to have Byzantine origins, were revealed as having come from Istanbul when a missing foot was discovered there in 1985. Similarly, the 'Pillars', two free-standing piers incised with vine and pomegranate decoration, are now known to have come from the church of Saint Polyeuktos in Constantinople, from which they were presumably removed shortly after 1204, together with capitals and other marbles. Originally, before the construction of the Cappella Zen, they framed the entrance to the Basilica at the south end of the west atrium. The legend connecting them to Acre is recounted by Sansovino, despite the presence of Greek monograms clearly indicating their place of origin, which presumably he was unable to read.

2. According to legend, these two carved piers on the south side of the
Basilica originally came from Acre. In reality they were brought from a
church in Constantinople, probably shortly after the Fourth Crusade of 1204.

Together with the many precious chalices, bookbindings, icons and other precious objects that fill the Treasury and Library of San Marco, the 'Pillars of Acre' and the 'Moors' are part of a rich haul of trophies brought from what had been the centre of power at the end of the first millennium, now redeployed as an index of Venice's new wealth and prestige. Significantly, in view of their position, yet further captured trophies, including marble panels and fragments of pulpits, are set into the external wall of the Treasury itself, as if to advertise its function as a storehouse of booty. Recent restoration of the north side of the Basilica has revealed to stunning effect the different textures and colours of this magnificent array of marbles and carvings, even if it is not so obviously a display of pillaged materials.

In terms of both language and style, the contrast between the north and south façades of the Basilica is great; it is also a gentle reminder that the main entrance to the square throughout the middle ages and into the early modern period was from the lagoon, and that the southern façade was the first aspect of the Basilica to be seen on arrival. Modern visitors enter the Piazza either from under the porticos which frame it, or from the bridges along the quayside and behind the Basilica, but the square was originally designed to be approached from the water. As the domain of the doge, who arrived in the *bucintoro*, the Piazza was planned to be ceremonially approached from this perspective. This also explains the counterintuitive orientation of the façade mosaics, whose original appearance can be seen in Bellini's painting. Designed to be read from right to left, they reflect the direction from which Mark's relics arrived from Alexandria to be received in the Doge's Palace. More importantly, the view from the lagoon also underlines that the south door, framed by the 'Pillars of Acre' before it was closed off by the construction of the Cappella Zen in 1504, was the main entrance to the Basilica from the Piazzetta. Close to the Ducal Palace, from where they are overlooked by a relief depicting the Judgement of Solomon, the 'Pillars' have been seen as a columnar preface to a building which, after the addition of the atria, now measured 100 royal cubits wide. It has been suggested that they were intended to recall the two piers known as Jachin and Boaz, wrought for King Solomon's temple in Jerusalem by Hiram of Tyre in the tenth century BCE, thus further reinforcing the Solomonic resonances of the western area of the Basilica. By way of these analogies, San Marco could be thought to assume the qualities of Constantinople itself, which through the importation of Christian relics and the establishment of sanctuaries and monasteries had constructed the image of a New Jerusalem. This new identity, superimposed upon the earlier one of Constantinople as the New Rome, encouraged the Venetians to present themselves in the twelfth and thirteenth centuries as the inheritors of Byzantium. As such, it reflected both the political and cultural importance of the Eastern empire for Venetian self-fashioning.

The main western front of the Basilica is a magisterial expression of dominion. Of all the façades this is the most coherent and the iconography of its carved reliefs follows a carefully planned scheme. This serves not only as a visual preface to the interior, but also to display Venetian power through a spectacular display of trophies and the images of local saints, crucially punctuated by the sculptural programme of the Last Judgement. The personifications of the virtues provide a religious and ethical element, while the introduction of the familiar medieval themes of the labours and the months serves to emphasise the importance of civic duty. The six plaques in the spandrels are a mixture of old and new; three come from Constantinople, while the remaining three were carved to match in Venice. As a series they make constant reference to the origins of Venice through images of the Archangel Gabriel and the Virgin, and to the two warrior saints George and Demetrius. Another late-antique relief shows Herakles delivering the Ermanthian boar to King Eurystheus, while a companion piece depicts Herakles carrying the Kerynitian hind while trampling the Hydra of Lerna underfoot. Since Eraclea, the earliest political centre in the lagoon and the seat of the first doge, had been named after him, this transforms a classical composition not merely into a Christian message, but also into a specifically Venetian one.

The most spectacular of all the trophies from Constantinople are, of course, the four bronze horses, displayed on eight short columns of white marble and four of porphyry, raised triumphantly on the loggia above the central portal and dramatically set against the dark central window. Having secured them (in Constantinople they probably adorned the Hippodrome), the Venetians were apparently not entirely sure what to do with them (one reported suggestion, apparently bogus, was that they should be melted down for cannons), and while decisions were made – characteristically taking half a century – they were stored in the Arsenal. From an early date they were gilded (at an early stage they were also equipped with silver bridles – the visual effect of gold and silver glistening in the sunlight must have been stunning), and they appear as such in Bellini's painting, as well as in the reports of early travellers and local antiquarians. Typical of such descriptions is Pietro Giustinian's *Rerum venetarum ab urbe condita historia* (1560), which speaks of 'four unbridled horses glistening with gold'; according to Giustinian they had been made by the Greek sculptor Lysippus and were then taken to Rome. The question of their pedigree has exercised historians since the early humanists first entered the debate. Were they Greek or Roman? Some wished them to be Roman work from the start. Cyriac of Ancona, one of the best informed and most scholarly early fifteenth-century students of antique marbles, having carefully measured them from rump to hoof, believed them to be the work of Phidias, regarded at the time as the greatest of Roman sculptors (he is now regarded as the most important fifth-century BC Greek sculptor who famously worked on the Parthenon marbles). In the early nineteenth century, following Lord Elgin's purchase of the Parthenon frieze and its arrival in London, opinion veered towards Greek origins; one writer who believed them to be Greek went so far as to compare one of the heads unfavourably with the famous Elgin horse. Later still, in the wake of the unification of Italy in the nineteenth century, the Risorgimento, it was reasserted that the horses were Roman, and therefore Italian. Whatever their origin, from Rome they travelled to Constantinople on the orders of the emperor, before finally fetching up in Venice as part of the spoils looted during the Fourth Crusade of 1199–1204. In effect this located the history of the horses within the evolving myth of imperial Venice as the successor to the two earlier empires of Rome and Byzantium, and as a visible and tangible proof of this genealogy; the Venetian capacity to claim descent from both was an important feature of an evolving myth of state. By planting the quadriga above the west door of the Basilica, its status as the spoils of war was underlined to those gathered in the square below. Possession and public display of the horses, the most politically charged of all the trophies brought to Venice after the collapse of Constantinople, made the doge if not the emperor (a title reserved for the count of Flanders) at least '*Dominator quartae et dimidae parties totius Romaniae*' ('Lord of a quarter and half a quarter of the Roman Empire'). During the early Middle Ages this potent phrase was delivered as the climax of a moment of emotive state ritual when the doge proclaimed his titles while standing between the horses on the balcony of the Basilica. It also provided the pretext for the claim that the city itself had become the new Byzantium, and that, having driven out its Greek masters, the Venetians were set to fulfil an historic mission as the true heirs of Constantine himself.

The symbolic significance of the horses may have been even greater than that. One recent reconstruction of their arrangement on the terrace of the façade suggests that they may have formed the culmination of a thematically integrated sculptural group consisting of the five reliefs of Christ and the Evangelists now set into the north façade, but previously placed in the second storey above the present position of the quadriga. If this reconstruction of the tympanum is correct, it encourages the association of the four horses and the four Evangelists with the metaphor of the Quadriga Domini, charged with spreading the Gospel throughout the entire world. In this interpretation the Basilica of San Marco, the repository of Mark's relics, becomes the point of departure for an historic mission, and the centre not only of the Venetian empire but also that of a proselytising enterprise of universal significance, directed from a favoured city inhabited by a Chosen People. That ambitious and politically charged idea, destined to reverberate throughout the following centuries, is also proclaimed by the overall scheme of the west façade, which juxtaposes episodes from the *translatio* with scenes from the New Testament beginning with marble reliefs of Mary and Gabriel, and continuing with four Christological scenes in the mosaic lunettes of the upper storey. The climax is reached with the central portal which shows the dead rising from their tombs while Christ, surrounded by angels, announces the Second Coming.

The determination of the Venetians to imitate Byzantium, in particular to rival the opulent interior of Justinian's church of the Holy Apostles, also influenced the mosaic decorations of the interior. Nothing could have prepared most visitors for the experience of first seeing them, particularly shimmering in candlelight, as was the case for much of their history. Some sense of that amazement comes through in the memoirs completed in 1498 of the French diplomat Philippe de Commynes, who was sent by Charles VIII to negotiate with the Venetians after the French armies crossed the Alps into Italy in 1494. For Commynes, the Basilica was 'the goodliest and richest Church in the world, bearing but the name of a chapel: for it is built throughout of the curious work called Mosaique or Marquetry; the art also whereof they vaunt themselves to be authors of'. As was appropriate for a great Italian city state, unrivalled as a sea power, late fifteenth-century Venice was, in Commynes' eyes, a resplendent city, nowhere more so than in the interior of San Marco.

Inside the Basilica, the mosaics which cover the walls, vaults and, above all, the five domes glimmered in the flickering light. This is the spectacle that impressed not only Commynes but every visitor to San Marco before and since. On ceremonial occasions, with the great Byzantine doors of the central entrance open, this scene would also have been visible to some of those standing in the Piazza. In general terms, and also in many details of their iconography, the mosaics are clearly indebted to Byzantine models. This was partly conditioned by the political and ecclesiastical policies of the Venetian state during the twelfth and thirteenth centuries, a time of consolidation and mythologising when the legends surrounding Saint Mark were extensively used to elaborate the foundation myth of Venice itself. Perhaps inevitably, the visual language chosen to express them was derived, as had been the plan of San Marco itself, from the example of Constantinople. Nowhere can this be more clearly seen than in the three major pictorial narratives of the Reception of Mark's Relics made during this period, all of them inside the Basilica.

Taken in sequence, the changing emphases of these works of art are testimony to the growth in Venetian ambition and authority in the world. The earliest is to be seen among the lower panels of the Pala d'Oro, the colossal gilt altarpiece still in the Basilica which was commissioned by Doge Ordelaffo Falier in Constantinople in the early twelfth century. The structure of Falier's altarpiece, which has remained essentially unaltered, is divided into two horizontal sections, with an upper part that was probably added in the early thirteenth century when the Pala was converted from an altar frontal into a screen. It consists of a dazzling display of angels, saints, prophets and apostles arranged in horizontal bands around the central figure of Christ enthroned. These are set into a massive silver-gilt frame ablaze with precious stones. Among the enamels which make up the lower section, a set of ten square panels portrays three scenes from the life of Mark.

3. The Pala d'Oro, decorated with enamels and precious stones, stands over the crypt which houses the body of Saint Mark. Adapted from an earlier altarpiece, and subsequently enlarged, it contains 187 plaques and 1,927 gems arranged in a silver-gilt frame.

The first group shows his mission to Aquileia, and the second that to Alexandria. The third, which brings the narrative to its climax, shows the *translatio*. In the first of this group, the body is shown being lifted from its tomb by Tribonus and Rusticus. In the following two scenes the men are portrayed accompanying the relics to Venice. Finally, the culmination of the sequence shows their reception against a background which includes a single-domed building, presumably the first church of San Marco. Here the body is displayed in an open coffin escorted by soldiers carrying lances. Heading the reception party is the bishop of Olivolo-Castello surrounded by a group of Venetian clergy rather than, as might be expected, the doge, who is significantly absent from both the image and the explanatory inscription placed above. This emphasis upon spiritual rather than temporal authority is consistent with Byzantine tradition, as is the overall impact of the Pala itself, which must have struck contemporary Venetians as not merely grand but decidedly imperial.

Just a few decades later, around the middle of the twelfth century, political realities shifted. In an imposing mosaic panel showing the *translatio* in the Cappella San Clemente, the doge now appears. The five patricians who accompany him are members of the *Consilium sapientium* (Council of Wise Men), the elected representatives of the Venetian people. This body, which was presided over by the doge, was the nucleus of what later became the Maggior Consiglio, or Great Council. Its presence in the scene, alongside the patriarch of Grado, the bishops of the area, the clergy of the city and the doge, transforms the iconography of the reception of the relics of Saint Mark into a magisterial statement of new political and commercial realities.

The determination to follow Byzantine example in many aspects of Venetian culture continued to be strong from the fall of Constantinople until the end of the Latin Kingdom. Symptomatic of the continuing pull of the image of Constantinople as the original 'new Rome' – an image which had long fascinated the Venetians in their quest for a sense of identity with ancient and distinguished roots – was the proposal, made in 1222, to transfer the seat of Venetian government to the shores of the Bosphorus. The trading advantages (including access to the ports of the Black Sea) which had come in the wake of the Fourth Crusade survived both the restoration of a Greek emperor and the Muslim reconquest of Syria. For the Venetians, as canny as ever in their business dealings with the East (Martin da Canal wrote that 'merchandise passes through this noble city as water flows through fountains'), these different political circumstances merely required commercial reorganisation. Trade with Constantinople and beyond continued despite the change of regime, Venetian maritime possessions flourished, and in 1261 Marco Polo's father and uncle vigorously pursued their trading operations as far as central Asia. Completed in the early years of the transitional period which marked the end of Venetian attachment to Byzantium and the more Roman-inspired imperial era which followed, the mosaic in the Cappella San Clemente, to the south of the High Altar, converts the *translatio* into an imposing statement about Venetian civic and ecclesiastical authority in the middle decades of the twelfth century.

The episode of the *translatio* is treated for the third time in the thirteenth-century mosaics on the west façade of the Basilica itself, where the reception of the body of Saint Mark occupies the lunette above the Porta Sant'Alipio. This is the only part of the original scheme to have survived; the mosaics over the remaining four doors, clearly legible in Bellini's depiction of the west front, were completely replaced in the later centuries. Read from right to left, the various episodes which make up the *translatio*, including the most recent addition, the *praedestinatio*, have now been expanded from the seven scenes shown in the Cappella San Clemente cycle to a grand total of thirteen; in the process, the transferral of Mark's relics to Venice is given much greater prominence than in the earlier narrative. Here they are shown being carried in solemn procession accompanied, as in the San Clemente mosaics, by the patriarch of Grado and the bishops under his jurisdiction.

The climax of the entire façade cycle occurs in the lunette of the Porta Sant'Alipio. Here, the richly dressed body of the saint, displayed in an open coffin, is being carried through the main door of the church by two clerics, one of whom can be identified as the patriarch of Grado. A crowd of men, women and children positioned to the left acclaim the arrival of Mark's body, while to the right the doge, dressed in full regalia, joins in the welcome. Surprisingly, none of this fits with the traditional version of the *translatio*. On the contrary, the scene shown in the lunette expands the reception of Mark's relics from a simple welcome to a formal ceremony, in which the principal representatives of Church and state are present in a magisterial gathering of more than forty-six people, including state officials, clerics and people. Read in conjunction with the previous mosaic in the façade cycle which, according to Bellini's *Procession* and later descriptions in guidebooks, originally showed the more traditional reception of Mark's body by a smaller gathering included the six bishops of Venetia, the Porta Sant'Alipio mosaic presents the arrival of Mark's body as a triumphal appropriation of his relics by the *commune veneciarum*. The Basilica itself is shown in its thirteenth-century form, with its domes completed, marble cladding added and the four horses in position. In effect, this is a dramatic and potent expression of the power of the Venetian state at a crucial moment in its history. Taken in their correct historical sequence, these three different interpretations of the *translatio* provide clear testimony to crucial shifts in the Venetian power structure, as the state itself took on more imperial dimensions. From the simple and informal gathering that receives Saint Mark's body in the Pala d'Oro panel, the scene expands in both majesty and size in the later versions of the scene, to reach an heroic climax in the Porta Sant'Alipio mosaic.

From this perspective, it comes as a surprise to realise that Venice had not always been the seat of government in the area. In the seventh century, Malamocco, now a quiet fishing village overlooking the lagoon, had been developed as an important episcopal and administrative centre, and it functioned in this way for some two hundred years until its operations were transferred to Venice itself. This inaugurates the history of the Ducal Palace, the other major medieval building in the Piazza, whose development is inevitably closely intertwined with that of the Basilica itself. During the dogeship of Agnello Particiaco in the early ninth century, the most important administrative and governmental offices of the state were established in Venice itself, and it was then that the first palace was constructed as the official residence of the doge and the chief magistrates of the city. Nothing survives either of this, said to have been burned down in 976, or of its successor, put up in the twelfth century during the dogeship of Sebastiano Ziani but subsequently rebuilt. The present south wing, instantly recognisable on account of its distinctive gothic façade decorated with a delicate pattern of white Istrian stone and pink Verona marble, dates from the fourteenth century. Begun in 1341, the focal point of this new palace was the construction of a new meeting hall for the Great Council (the Sala del Maggior Consiglio). Following the *serrata* ('closure') of the Great Council in 1297, membership of this governing body of the state was restricted to the patrician class, a mixture of aristocrats and merchants who inherited the right to participate in the government of the Republic on reaching the age of twenty-five. Some decades later, the Council voted funds to construct a meeting hall overlooking the Bacino di San Marco, which was large enough to hold its 1,212 members (the number was to increase even further in the following decades). These arrangements were further formalised in the sixteenth century by the introduction of the *Libro d'oro* (*The Golden Book*), in which the names of those entitled to serve in government were entered. Initially the *Libro d'oro* was a closed volume; neither donations nor bribes, however large, nor devotion to the Republic, however selfless or heroic, could gain entry for those whose families had been excluded at the time of the *serrata*. Later, during the 1600s, aspiring nobles were allowed to buy their way in. In essence, the Maggior Consiglio functioned as the main electorate of Venice, with the power to select magistrates who occupied the various administrative and judicial offices of state, usually for short terms of a year or even a few months. Some elections also took place in the Senate. While the system was designed to avoid factionalism and the concentration of power in too few hands, the price that had to be paid was a machine that worked only imperfectly.

With the Sala del Maggior Consiglio located at the west end of the wing overlooking the lagoon, the internal disposition of rooms within the palace reflects the structures of rule. Beginning in the sixteenth century with Donato Giannotti, whose influential treatise on the Venetian constitution was first published in 1540, descriptions of the system often liken it to a neat pyramid. At its base was the Great Council, above which came the Senate (which was itself divided into a number of distinct groups), while at the summit stood the Signoria, which consisted of the doge and six councillors together with the three heads of the Forty. Tidy as this might sound in theory, in reality the arrangement was cumbersome, its processes bedevilled by inefficiency, confusion and bureaucratic disorder. While the Maggior Consiglio may have been the sovereign body of state, and the distribution point for all offices and honours, in practice its size (by the sixteenth century it had grown to 2,500 members) meant that it could not deal effectively with day-to-day affairs. Rather it was the Senate that had real control over the details of government. More precisely, the locus of power and action was the Collegio, a much smaller body within the Senate, which acted as a sort of steering group. Sir Henry Wotton (1568–1639), the English ambassador to Venice in the early seventeenth century, quaintly described the Collegio as 'that member of the state, where (as in the stomach) all things are first digested'. In practice, there was a considerable distance between the much-vaunted virtues of a republican system and the near-oligarchical reality in which power was concentrated in the hands of a few powerful clans. The third element of the pyramid, the Signoria, organised the business of the Maggior Consiglio, but it was otherwise confined to a largely ceremonial role. Lying outside the main structure of government was the Council of Ten (Consiglio dei Dieci), which actually consisted of seventeen members including the Signoria. Its prime responsibility could be politely described as state security; in practice it functioned as the most powerful arm of the Venetian secret police. Constant collaboration and exchange of information between these various bodies was essential if any semblance of administrative order was to be sustained. Chaos, fed by factionalism, was sometimes not far away.

This structure is reflected in the disposition of the internal spaces of the Ducal Palace. Beginning with the Great Council itself, all the major official bodies were allocated rooms in which to meet and conduct business, an arrangement still evident in the present, much altered building. In addition there were the doge's private apartments, a gentle reminder that the palace was not a monarchical palace in the traditional sense, but a governmental centre which incorporated the residence of the head of state. The first phase of construction, which was concentrated on the new meeting hall, was more or less finished by 1365. Then there was a pause. The imposing central balconied window that punctuates the lagoon side of the building, built by Pier Paolo di Jacopo Dalle Masegne, is dated 1404, but it was not until fifteen years later that the chamber was finished and the Council met in its new home for the first time. Carved reliefs decorate the external corners of this elevation – the drunkenness of Noah near the Ponte della Paglia (with the figure of the Archangel Raphael in the loggia above), and Adam and Eve (surmounted by the

Archangel Michael) on the corner closest to the Piazzetta. These are clear statements of the importance of the Christian faith for the administration of good government. This wing of the palace was finally inaugurated in 1419, but a few years later the decision was taken to demolish the ancient law courts on the adjoining site to the north, and to extend the building, in the same style and using similar building materials, in the direction of the Basilica. The sixteenth-century balconied window in the centre of the new west façade was designed to echo Dalle Masegne's window in the lagoon façade, and the third and final corner relief of the newly extended building, showing the Judgement of Solomon with the Archangel Gabriel in the loggia above, was added.

In a further attempt to make this elevation resonate with the themes and iconography of the lagoon façade, the west façade incorporates a roundel framing a sculpted figure of Venecia, the female personification of the Republic itself, executed about the middle of the fourteenth century, probably carved by Filippo Calendario. Here she is shown crowned and seated upon a Solomonic throne of lions, holding a sword in her right hand. In this way the symbolic figure of Venecia is presented as a modified figure of Justice, in an iconographical configuration in which the state is inextricably fused with the concept of just government. As if to remove any possible doubt about this message and its political dimensions, the scroll in her left hand, visible for all to see from ground level, reads: '*Fortis / Iusta / Trono / Furias / Mare / Sub Pede / Pono*' ('Enthroned just and strong, I defeat the furies by sea'). The isolated personification of Justice, familiar enough in the visual rhetoric of the communes of late medieval Italy (as Ambrogio Lorenzetti's frescoes of Good Government and

4. The female personification of Venice looks down on the Piazzetta from the west façade of the Ducal Palace. Beneath her gaze, criminals were executed between the two pillars at the edge of the lagoon.

Bad Government (*c.* 1328) in the Palazzo Pubblico in Siena remind us), also appears on the top of Dalle Masegne's balconied window on the south side of the Ducal Palace. Here she is presented as a free-standing statue, authoritative and imposing. But in Calendario's roundel, Justice is conflated with the image of the Virgin Mary enthroned so as to construct an even more powerful statement through a specific reference to Venetian domination of the seas. As such it is among the earliest examples of civic imagery capitalising on Marian iconography.

This component of Calendario's roundel underlines the important role that the Virgin played in Venetian state theology through her long-standing association with the city. In addition to being constantly reminded of the local resonances of the cult of the Madonna through the annual liturgical cycle, the inhabitants of Venice were everywhere confronted by Marian images. Worshipped in shrines in *calle* and *campo*, and commemorated as protectress in stone reliefs and statues, the Virgin was a constant presence in the everyday lives of ordinary Venetians. For citizens of all social classes, her comforting image carried a quite precise political and civic message that was intimately connected to the origins, evolution and future of the Republic.

In much of official rhetoric, Venice was represented to the outside world as a pure, uncorrupted virgin state, unwalled and without gates, yet unconquered for more than a thousand years, a city unviolated by outside forces. In this way, popular religious devotion and the categorisation of the city as a special protectorate of the Virgin fed into the notion of uniqueness and perfection which lies at the heart of the 'Myth of Venice' so eloquently delineated by Petrarch in his famous description of the city as 'the one home today of liberty, peace and justice, the one refuge of honourable men, the one port to which can repair the storm-tossed, tyrant-hounded craft of men who seek the good life'. It was also supported by popular belief since, according to the legend established by Jacopo Dondi's chronicle, Venice had been founded on the feast of the Annunciation; in consequence the city also assumed the attributes of the Virgin, in particular her purity and immortality. This was in turn coupled with the historical reality that, unlike most other Italian states, Venice had not been invaded by foreigners. When Charles VIII of France descended on Italy in 1494, bringing with him an army infested with syphilis (at least according to Italian popular belief, which promptly christened the disease the *mal francese*), Venice remained comparatively unscathed by the invasion (though the disease itself certainly arrived). During the summer of 1513, when the whole of the *terraferma* was occupied by the forces of the League of Cambrai and the nearby town of Mestre was set on fire, the enemy troops fell short of crossing the lagoon and besieging the city. In 1527 Rome itself was occupied by legions of a half-savage Lutheran soldiery and the pope was forced to flee, while in Florence the republican regime collapsed after the city was besieged by imperial troops. It is hardly surprising that for Venetians living in the first half of the sixteenth century, contemporary events only seemed to confirm the special status of Venice as a divinely protected entity.

In practice the idea was not new, as Petrarch's words remind us. The theme of the Virgin as the protectress of Venice, common enough in the period, occurs in the central moment of Guariento di Arpo's (*c.* 1310–70) magisterial fresco of the

Coronation of the Virgin in Paradise, of which only fragments now survive, which originally decorated the tribune wall of the Sala del Maggior Consiglio. The political message of the scene is made explicit through the large number of attendant figures, while the presence of the Virgin together with that of the Archangel Gabriel recall once again the legend of the foundation of the city on the feast of the Annunciation. Commissioned by Doge Marco Cornaro and painted shortly after 1365, Guariento's *Coronation* was severely damaged in the fire which devastated the Ducal Palace in 1577. The task of replacing it was originally assigned to Paolo Veronese (1528–88), but work was never begun and, after the artist's death, the commission was given to Jacopo Tintoretto (1518–94), whose vast *Paradise* canvas, executed between the years 1588 and 1592, and completed by his son Domenico, employs a similar iconographical scheme.

The inner courtyard of the Doge's Palace is in a mixture of styles. Antonio Rizzo (*c.* 1440–99), a sculptor, architect and engineer from Verona who also worked inside the Basilica, was responsible for the east side, the northern part of which was rebuilt after the fire of 1483 which destroyed several parts of the complex. It was Rizzo who constructed the Scala dei Giganti, a grand ceremonial staircase leading to the entrance to the Doge's Palace. Traditionally used as a balcony where foreign ambassadors could be received, it was also the place where the newly elected doge received his traditional ceremonial *corno*, or cap, during his investiture. Later the staircase was framed by Jacopo Sansovino's huge marble statues of Mars and Neptune (hence its name), symbols of Venetian territorial and maritime power. The southern side of the courtyard was completed in the middle of the sixteenth century, while the lower storeys of the remaining two sides were finished in the same manner in the seventeenth. Projecting into the central space from the west is the Arco Foscari. Modelled on a classical triumphal arch, this was begun in the fifteenth century but was completed only towards the end of the sixteenth, when the imposing statue of Francesco Maria I della Rovere, duke of Urbino (1490–1538), was added to the already rich ensemble of sculptures. This is consonant with the themes of Sansovino's monumental statues; della Rovere, a military strategist and expert on fortifications, was employed by the Venetians to advise on the defence of its territories.

On 11 May 1574, a fire broke out in an upstairs kitchen of the Doge's Palace during a banquet being held by Doge Alvise Mocenigo to mark the fourth anniversary of his election. Fanned by the wind, the flames spread quickly and destroyed gilded ceilings and some of the most important and monumental pictures in six rooms of the official apartments. A programme of restoration was quickly put in hand, but some three years later an even more serious conflagration occurred; this time paintings by Bellini, Alvise Vivarini, Vittore Carpaccio, Titian, Veronese and Tintoretto were all lost, while Guariento's great *Paradise* fresco in the Sala del Maggior Consiglio was also badly damaged, effectively beyond repair. Interestingly, it was decided not to replace the damaged building but to restore it, a sign perhaps of its iconic significance. The iconographical content of the new decorative scheme of the meeting room of the Great Council, commissioned from the leading Venetian artists of the day, was worked out by a Benedictine monk, Fra Girolamo Bardi. As executed, most of the paintings show important Venetian military and naval achievements, individual doges and allegories of the benefits of Venetian government. Those on the side walls, executed in the years 1578–95, show three significant moments in Venetian history: the legendary meeting in 1177 between Holy Roman Emperor Frederick I Barbarossa and Pope Alexander III, the capture of Constantinople during the Fourth Crusade in 1204, and the Venetian victory at the battle of Chioggia in 1381.

The entire cycle is brought to a triumphant conclusion by three large-scale allegories, on the ceiling, painted in 1578–95, all of which show Venice in her traditional female personification in the act of being crowned. In Palma Il Giovane's *Triumph of Venice* she is surrounded by the trophies of war, while in Veronese's *Apotheosis* she is accompanied by a squadron of allegorical figures – Peace, Abundance, Fame, Felicity, Security, Honour and Liberty. The third canvas in the sequence, Tintoretto's depiction of *The Senate Receiving the Submission of the Provinces* presents Venetia together with the Lion of Saint Mark offering a palm branch and an olive wreath, the symbols of victory and peace, to the doge. Based on ancient Roman imagery, the rhetoric of these grandiloquent visual statements of Venetian self-glorification at the end of the sixteenth century has a long history.

3

....

THE NEW ROME

'You are the man who knows how to be Vitruvius'
                    Pietro Aretino in a letter to Jacopo Sansovino

In common with many other northern Italian cities that benefited from the trade routes between the eastern Mediterranean and Europe, Venice expanded and prospered between
the eleventh and the fourteenth centuries. Initially, urban
development was concentrated in the two ecclesiastical and
political centres of the growing city: the island of Olivolo,
which had succeeded Malamocco as the seat of the bishop
of Venice as early as the eighth century; and the area around
the church of San Marco. It was while Contarini's church
was being constructed, during the second half of the eleventh
century, that Piazza San Marco began to be given a greater
sense of official purpose and, in consequence, a more formal
appearance. Originally the space directly in front of the Basilica had been somewhat rustic in aspect, being made up of two
islands separated by a canal. At this time the eastern end of
the site was occupied by the Ducal Palace and the Basilica,
while a free-standing bell tower (originally built as a forti-
fication) stood among the cluster of buildings that framed
it. These included shops, houses and a hospice for pilgrims

who had come to Venice to venerate the relics of Saint Mark, as well as those of the many saints housed elsewhere in the city, and sometimes to make the dangerous if spiritually prestigious journey to the Holy Land. An L-shaped open field, which ran towards the lagoon in one direction and away from San Marco in the other, and which had been traditionally used as a meeting place for the discussion of matters of state, was now remodelled. The most important feature of this renovation was the construction of a ribbon of houses, all of the same height, with shops on the ground floor, around its northern, southern and western boundaries. This, which not only gave the area a more official and ordered inflection but also established the characteristic mixture of functions that it still retains, probably took place during the dogeship of Sebastiano Ziani in the 1170s. As a result, it seems likely that by the end of the twelfth century, both the shape and character of the Piazza and its associated Piazzetta as they remained until the end of the Republic had been effectively established. With Doge Ziani's modifications in place, the Piazza now functioned properly as an imposing forecourt to San Marco to which it was both visually and ceremonially connected. Taken together, the total area of both the Piazza and Piazzetta was greater than that of any of the squares of mainland Italian cities, including Bologna, Florence and Siena. Finally paved in brick in 1266, the new ensemble was now complete.

The changes carried out during Ziani's dogeship are characteristic of a more general approach to the urban fabric of late twelfth-century Venice. As the self-confidence of the commune grew, so it increasingly assumed control of any significant alterations to the public areas (responsibility for which had previously been in the hands of individual citizens), ordering and embellishing the focal points of civic and religious life with appropriate structures. The transformation of the open area in front of the church into what was effectively a new and imposing civic space was one of three major projects carried out by the Venetian authorities during the period; the other two were the development of the area around the Rialto bridge as the principal trading centre of the city, and the reconstruction of the naval dockyard (the Arsenal), which was destined to become the largest industrial complex in medieval Europe. Taken as a whole, these three ambitious initiatives signalled a determination to embellish the principal sites of the military, commercial and politico-ecclesiastical life of Venice.

It was as part of this philosophy that the Doge's Palace was enlarged, and that a number of other changes were made to the surrounding area. At the water's edge two granite columns, which later supported sculpted figures of the Lion of Saint Mark and Saint Theodore, were placed so as to form an entrance to the Piazzetta from the lagoon. This arrangement also followed the practice, familiar from Roman imperial example, of displaying statues on columns as symbols of authority. These two were later joined by a number of other free-standing columns, including the 'Pillars of Acre'. The presence nearby of Calendario's roundel incorporating the image of Venecia/Justice on the façade of the palace is a reminder that in the Piazzetta, under her watchful gaze, those found guilty of severe crimes were executed between the two columns. Continuing the theme of the fundamental role of justice in a well-ordered society, laws and decrees were proclaimed from the nearby Pietra del Bando, and it was there that the heads of traitors were also displayed, 'though the smell of them doth breede a very offensive and contagious annoyance', as the seventeenth-century English visitor Thomas Coryate put it. The overall implication is clear. Both the Basilica and the Ducal Palace are to be considered as Solomonic structures, appropriate for the concept of Venice as the New Jerusalem, a notion which is itself clearly modelled on the precedent of Constantinople.

The same idea was also evident in some of the rituals that were enacted in both the Basilica and the Piazza on the major feast days of the Christian year. During the Easter morning ceremonies in San Marco, the doge processed to the Easter Sepulchre (a temporary structure made for the occasion), where the '*Quem Queritis?*' ('Whom Do You Seek?') was sung. Performed throughout the Western church, this consisted of a four-sentence exchange between Mary the Mother of God, Mary Magdalene and Mary the sister of Lazarus, whom Jesus had raised from the dead. Its purpose was to recount the New Testament episode in which the three women went to the sepulchre after the Crucifixion, only to find it empty. In Venice, the '*Quem Queritis?*' was sung according to a local practice, which focused on the participation of the doge as the principal witness to the Resurrection. Outside in the Piazza, analogies between Venice and Jerusalem were also strongly evoked on the feast of Corpus Christi, when, having celebrated Mass in San Marco, some of the pilgrims who had gathered in the city to make the trip to the Holy Land walked in solemn procession around the square.

In some ways Piazza San Marco had more in common with imperial *fora* than with civic architecture elsewhere in Italy. As with the Basilica itself, the prime source of inspiration was Constantinople, where a sequence of forum-like squares, surrounded by meeting halls, public baths, shops, churches and palaces all linked by porticos, are strung out along the Mese, the city's principal thoroughfare. While the church of the Holy Apostles provided the Venetians with an architectural model which emphasised the status of San Marco as an apostolic foundation, so too the reconstruction of the Piazza along the lines of the Mese, which had been used as the route for victory processions, supplied an obvious imperial metaphor. In this context, the important modifications to the square made during the dogeship of Sebastiano Ziani were simply intended to dignify the official image and functions of the state. Later changes, carried out under Ziani's son Doge Pietro in the early thirteenth century, not only further amplified the Piazza and enlarged its stock of imperial references, but also made it more scenographic. As a result of clearances, the Basilica was now located more centrally along the eastern side of the square, and the Campanile appeared more obviously as a free-standing structure. Although this created a more spectacular setting for public ceremonial, the Doge's Palace was not visible from the far end of the Piazza since the Campanile was still surrounded on two sides by other buildings.

The heightened theatricality with which official processions could be held in the newly expanded Piazza was almost immediately put to use. According to Francesco Sansovino (1521–86), the demolition of the medieval church of San Geminiano on the western flank of the Piazza caused tension between Venice and the papacy which was only resolved by the invention of a new piece of ritual. One of a number of parishes that abutted on to the square (San Basso, a now deconsecrated church facing the north façade of the Basilica in the Piazzetta dei Leoncini is another), San Geminiano came under the direct control (*ius patronatus*) of the doge rather than that of the patriarch of Venice. None the less, the pope's displeasure at the demolition of San Geminiano caused Sebastiano Ziani to promise that an *andata* to a new church, which was to be rebuilt further to the west, be held annually. Giovanni Stringa, canon of San Marco, who recounted the details of the procession in its early seventeenth-century form, implies that it was an elaborate occasion which involved not only the doge, but also the Apostolic Legate (the official representative of the Holy See) and other dignitaries, together with the entire Signoria. On reaching the church, Mass was celebrated with music sung by the choir of San Marco. Returning to the Basilica, the complete ceremonial apparatus halted on the site of the earlier church; here the celebrant recounted the origins of the procession and formally issued an invitation to the doge to continue the practice in the following year. At a more symbolic level, the procession connected the two churches at either end of the Piazza: San Marco, large and magnificent, and San Geminiano, a small parish church. The dynamic tension between the two was finally resolved with the demolition of San Geminiano in the early nineteenth century.

Ziani's amplification of the Piazza gave it a form which was retained more or less unchanged until the early sixteenth century. Some idea of how it looked then is provided by two famous views of about the same date: Gentile Bellini's *Procession in Piazza San Marco* of 1496 and Jacopo de' Barbari's highly detailed bird's-eye view of the entire city published four years later. The map, printed in sections and in scale reminiscent of a mural, is the largest and most detailed plan of Venice to be produced before modern times; it is also of exceptional technical quality. Taken together, its six component sheets present a view of the city seen from the southwest, with the Alps visible on the horizon and the islands of the lagoon in the distance. Yet despite its naturalism and high level of detail, the real subject of the map is not only the physical city but also the economic power of the commonwealth of Venice. De' Barbari's map is in essence the earliest cartographical expression of the Myth of Venice, even if, in practice, it contains a number of important omissions and distortions. So too does Bellini's painting (where the Campanile, for example, has been moved to the south to allow the Porta della Carta to be seen); conventionally considered to be an almost archaeological record of how the square looked at the end of the Quattrocento, its accuracy is also compromised by extensive nineteenth-century restorations to the paint surface. Both of these images, produced so remarkably close to each other in time, show on both the north and the south sides of the Piazza a hotchpotch of gothic, romanesque and Renaissance buildings connected by the porticos which had been such a prominent aspect of the square since Ziani's twelfth-century enlargement. The map in particular gives a good account of the dimensions of the Piazza; the square then corresponded to its present length and width at its west end, but narrower towards San Marco.

With the important exception of the Procuratie Vecchie, the range of dwellings built for the procurators on the north side of the Piazza, both Bellini's painting and de' Barbari's map record how the square looked before Jacopo Sansovino began his ambitious scheme of renovation and reconstruction

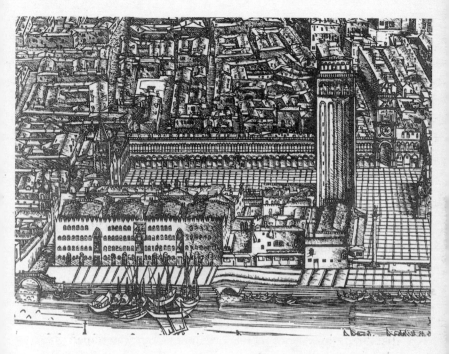

5. Jacopo de' Barbari's *View of Venice* of 1500, a monumental bird's-eye view of the entire city and the lagoon shows the Piazza, the Piazzetta and the buildings which adjoin them before Jacopo Sansovino's extensive remodelling of the area.

in the 1530s. Both include Mauro Codussi's elegant Torre dell'Orologio, or clocktower, at the entrance to the Merceria, the principal commercial artery of the city, which apart from its architectural qualities was also a piece of political bluff. Begun in 1496, when the Republic was close to insolvency (its financial resources had been severely drained by the continuing war against Naples), the decision to carry on building the Torre dell'Orologio was intended to deceive the rest of Italy into accepting that Venice was financially secure, and that its power was undiminished. Officially unveiled by Doge Agostino Barbarigo in 1499, it is crowned with two mechanised bell-jacks popularly known as 'the Moors'. Early in their history they were thought of as two giants ('*li doi ziganti*'), and it was only later, as the patina of the bronze darkened, that they received a more exotic, eastern descriptive tag. But their physiognomy indicates that they are savages, wild men from the woods, and clearly Caucasian. The Torre dell'Orologio was not merely ornamental but functioned as a marker of the passage of mercantile and civic time. With its state-of-the-art mechanism, constructed in 1493–9 by Giampaolo Rainieri and his son Zuan Carlo from Reggio Emilia, two of the most celebrated clockmakers of the day, it also dramatically shifted the Piazza into the realms of modern scientific time. Acclaimed by contemporaries as the most complex astronomical clock in existence (its painted and gilded clockface shows not only the hours in Roman numerals, but also the signs of the zodiac and their constellations and the phases of the moon), it provides a technological counterpoint to the medieval marking of time from the Campanile. For the efficient functioning of the elaborately choreographed processions in the square of precisely the kind of shown in Gentile

Bellini's *Procession*, it was crucial, while on an everyday basis it was an insistent feature of the soundscape.

So too was the Campanile. Perhaps the most recognisable symbol of Venice, it is at the same time the least discussed of all the buildings in the square. In part this is because of its troubled history, since to a greater extent than any other element of the Piazza, it has been endlessly reconstructed and restored over the centuries. Originally built in the ninth century, the Campanile doubled as a military watchtower. Later, as the structure was enlarged, the roof was sheathed in bronze so that it could function as a daytime beacon for mariners. It houses five bells in the belfry, which is topped by an attic faced in brick, the alternate faces of which show the Lion of Saint Mark and the figure of Venecia/Justice. These simple images insert the tower into the scheme of the square not only iconographically but also in terms of function (the bells summoned the citizenry to the Piazza on important occasions, both religious and civic). More precisely, each of the five had a specific purpose. The Renghiera (or Maleficio) announced executions in the Piazzetta, the Mezza Terza inaugurated a session of the Senate, the Nona marked midday, the Trottiera proclaimed a meeting of the Maggior Consiglio, and the Maragona sounded out the start and finish of the working day. Events of major significance in the life of the Republic, such as the death of the doge or news of military or naval victories, were also rung out from the tower. Following damage caused by an earthquake in 1511, the tower assumed its present form as a result of work carried out by Bartolomeo Bon (fl. 1421–64), who added the belfry, the attic and the spire surmounted by a gilded wooden statue of the Archangel Gabriel.

The Procuratie Vecchie, also built by 'Maistro Bon', was constructed at about the same time. Following the destruction of a range of Veneto-Byzantine houses on the north side of the square as the result of a fire in 1512, the procurators approved a plan which involved the construction of a new wing. Bon's building, eclectic and even anachronistic in style, breathes a spirit of continuity with Venetian architectural traditions, mainly through its deployment of repetitive arcading, whose rhythm provides the perfect backdrop for the processions and other official ceremonies that take place in the Piazza. The building not only recalled the previous configuration on this side of the square, but also contributed to the more widespread neo-Byzantine architectural revival which took place in Venice during the late fifteenth and early sixteenth centuries. Encouraged by a sequence of historically significant events, including the unification of the Eastern and Western churches after the Council of Florence in 1439 and the peace with the Sultan forty years later, the Venetians capitalised upon a distinct architectural style which consciously evoked past glories. Once again, the image was of the city as the successor to Constantinople itself.

Above all, the construction of the Procuratie Vecchie, like that of the Torre dell' Orologio, had a political and propagandistic dimension. In all probability this ambitious scheme to completely remodel the north side of the Piazza was in reaction to the battle of Agnadello in 1509, when the 20,000-strong Venetian army was decisively routed by the forces of the League of Cambrai, an alliance of the Pope and the Emperor, the kings of France, Aragon and Hungary, and the rulers of Mantua and Ferrara. Ever since the French had invaded Italy in 1494 the Venetians had tried to benefit from

6. Originally built in the twelfth century, the Procuratie Vecchie was reconstructed in a Veneto-Byzantine style in the early sixteenth. Its arrangement of porticos (fifty in total) with rooms above provided the template for Sansovino's Procuratie Vecchie on the south side of the Piazza and for his library building in the Piazzetta.

the uncertainty caused by the shifting balance of power, until the inevitable coalition was formed against them. For the diarist Girolamo Priuli (1476–1547), the disaster at Agnadello was to be blamed on a corrupt and degenerate aristocracy, a sinful citizenry, sexual licence in convents and monasteries, and sodomy and irreligion everywhere; in other words, behind the event could be detected the avenging Hand of God. In his *Istorie fiorentine*, published in 1532, Niccolò Machiavelli (1469–1527), advanced a more historically based explanation:

> *Whilst they lived in this way their name became dreaded at sea and respected within the confines of Italy. As time went on, the Venetians, impelled by the lust of dominion, seized Padua, Vicenza, Treviso, and, later on, Verona, Brescia, and Bergamo, besides many cities in Romagna, and the kingdom of Naples, and their renown increased so greatly that not only to the princes of Italy but to the sovereigns beyond the Alps they became objects of fear. Hence a conspiracy was formed against them, and in one day they lost that dominion which with infinite pains they had built up during many years. Although in recent years they have regained some part of it, they have never recovered their former renown or power, and they live at the discretion of others, as do all other Italian principalities.*

As Machiavelli realised, after Agnadello the Venetians were more exposed and vulnerable than they had been in their entire history. Petrarch's trope of 'unwalled and yet unconquered' had almost come to grief as the enemy troops put Mestre to the torch but then stopped short of Venice itself. Certainly Machiavelli's keen assessment of the political realities of the Venetian situation in the post-Agnadello world strikes a realistic note. Seen in these terms, many details of the sixteenth-century redevelopment of the Piazza constitute a determined effort to assert a somewhat idealised image of the place of the Republic in international affairs. Bon's Procuratie Vecchie, designed at a moment when Venetian alignment with its Byzantine past was once again briefly in vogue in the search for a distinct and independent architectural voice, inaugurates the first phase of one of the most distinctive architectural features of the square, the two facing ranges of procuracy buildings on its north and south sides. That, at least, is how they appeared to many visitors. Coryate, for example, thought that 'these two rowes are the principall things that beautifie St Mark's place', and noted the functional separation between the two storeys of the building: 'the upper part whereof containeth the dwelling houses of some of the Clarissimoes and Gentlemen of the citie, the lower part the houses of artificers and mechanical men that keepe their shops there'. Coryate's 'Clarissimoes and Gentlemen' were the procurators. Holders of one of the most ancient offices in the Venetian constitution, these powerful officials, elected for life, were second only to the doge in terms of status and influence. From the beginning of their long history, they had made detailed decisions about artistic matters; it was the procurators of San Marco (there were others responsible for other areas of the city) who oversaw the programme of mosaic work in the Basilica, the procurators who appointed the chapel master in charge of the choir, and the procurators who were responsible for the appearance and upkeep of the Piazza.

Jacopo Sansovino was made *proto magister* (chief architect) to the procurators of San Marco in 1529, two years after having arrived in Venice *en route* for France as a refugee from the Sack of Rome two years earlier, when the Eternal City was devastated by the mutinous troops of Holy Roman Emperor Charles V. Doge Andrea Gritti had noticed Sansovino's talents, and had arranged for him to be given the task of supervising the repair of the cupolas of the Basilica. This had evidently gone well, and on the death of the previous *proto*, Pietro Bon, Sansovino was the preferred candidate to succeed him. This put him in charge of nearly all new construction and repair work in the Piazza, including the Basilica but excluding the Ducal Palace which came under the direct jurisdiction of the doge. He was also responsible, on a day-to-day basis, for the maintenance of all properties owned and administered by the procurators elsewhere in the city, as on the *terraferma*. This placed Sansovino in the enviable postion of being employed by the wealthiest patrons of new building work anywhere in Venice, at a time when the political will to remodel the Piazza was strong. Although Gritti was undoubtedly the main political force behind the overall scheme, the overseers of the work on a daily basis were the procurators who lived in the square (as did Sansovino himself), and whose decisions are recorded.

The consequence was a spectacular large-scale *renovatio urbis*, begun during Gritti's dogeship and pursued, despite some economic setbacks, with his unswerving enthusiasm for this, the grandest of all the various projects that he encouraged while in power. After the trauma of Agnadello, and the loss of Venetian prestige which followed, Gritti's aim was to restore confidence in the city as a great international entrepôt flourishing once again under the benign administration of a model republican regime. Physical expression of this concept was to be secured through a radical architectural renewal of the central civic spaces at San Marco and the Rialto, in order to lend them an appropriate sense of splendour, modernity, magnificence and *auctoritas*. Venetian interest in Roman architectural style, often associated with the diaspora that followed the Sack, had been advocated by Gritti from shortly after his election in 1523. Sansovino, whose second period of residence in Rome essentially lasted from 1518 to 1527 (there were short intermissions in Florence and possibly in Venice), was the agent through whom Gritti's plan was to be realised.

As it unfolded, Sansovino's task was not merely to complete Bon's unfinished Procuratie Vecchie, but also to inaugurate the first phase of a grandiose plan to line the remaining sides of the Piazza and the Piazzetta, together with the eastern end of the landing quay, the Molo, with new structures. According to Francesco Sansovino, his father believed that the Piazza was the most dignified public space of any city in Italy, and had decided that it should be ornamented with buildings that, following ancient practice, were to be adorned with models of the classical style 'full of columns, friezes and cornices'; the intention was to superimpose a visual layer of ancient Rome upon the existing Byzantine elements. The result represents not only an attempt to articulate the Myth of Venice in appropriate architectural terms but also as a brave reinterpretation on a magisterial scale of the plan of the ancient Roman forum as described by Vitruvius in his *Ten Books of Architecture* from the first century BC, the only significant architectural treatise to have survived from classical antiquity. Fra Giocondo's celebrated illustrated edition of Vitruvius, published in Venice in 1511, during the War of the League of Cambrai, had aroused some interest in classical monuments, but it was not until the arrival of Sansovino – who had studied the ruins *in situ* during his Roman years – that the precepts were put into practice. The importance of Sansovino's advocacy of the new style is made explicit in Daniele Barbaro's commentaries on the *Ten Books*, published in Venice in 1556 with illustrations by the architect Andrea Palladio (1508–80), where each of Vitruvius's building types are matched to Venetian examples in general, and to Sansovino's work in the Piazza in particular.

When Sansovino started work on the square, its southern flank still preserved its ancient Veneto-Byzantine buildings; they can be clearly seen in Bellini's painting (see illustration 1) and, somewhat less clearly, in Jacopo de' Barbari's view (see illustration 5). Among them was the Ospizio Orseolo (a hostel for pilgrims) at the foot of the Campanile, the bell tower itself, which lay along the same axis, and the houses in which the procurators lived. Temporary shacks for money-changing were propped up against the bell tower, and bakers sold their bread from nearby stalls. According to Sansovino's fellow Florentine, the artist and architect Giorgio Vasari (1511–74):

> *In the year 1529 there were butchers' stalls between the two columns of the Piazza, with a number of small wooden booths, used for the vilest purposes, and a shame as well as deformity to the place, offending the dignity of the Palace and the Piazza, while they could not but disgust all strangers who made their entry into Venice, by the side of San Giorgio.*

The decrepit conditions on this side of the square, painfully obvious to those procurators who lived there, must have been thrown into stark relief by the completion of Bon's Procuratie

Vecchie directly opposite. In 1535 the decision to rebuild was taken. Sansovino, commissioned to design a new building to house the procurators, proposed a two-storey wing of apartments with shops on the ground floor, running from the Campanile to the church of San Geminiano on the western edge of the Piazza. In the event this scheme, clearly intended to echo Bon's wing though in a more classical register, was not begun immediately, and early in 1537 construction started instead on a new building facing the Doge's Palace in the Piazzetta. It seems that the procurators had finally decided that the priority was to house Cardinal Basilios Bessarion's unrivalled collection of ancient Greek and Latin manuscripts, which had been bequeathed by him to the Republic in 1468, but which embarrassingly had remained without a proper home ever since.

Bessarion (1403–72), a Greek bishop of formidable learning, had played a major role in the intellectual life of late fifteenth-century Venice. Earlier he had been a prominent figure in the church Councils of Ferrara and Florence, and was subsequently created a cardinal by Pope Eugenius IV (1383–1447), who saw him as the ideal mediator between the Greek and Latin churches. Although he never returned to his native country after his arrival at the Papal Court in 1440, Bessarion lobbied intensively for a co-ordinated crusade to recover Constantinople from the Turks, but, despite embassies to Naples, Germany, Venice and France conducted over a fifteen-year period, he failed to raise the necessary support. Determined to salvage what he could of the Greek literary heritage, Bessarion assembled a formidable library of Greek manuscripts to which he then added an important collection of Latin books.

Bessarion's donation had been made on condition that suitable accommodation for his library should be found somewhere close to the Basilica, and that the books should be made available for consultation by scholars. Over decades of indecision, the library had been moved from one temporary location to another, with some volumes being damaged in transit and others lost. Following the fall of Constantinople in 1453, Venice had become a major centre for Greek intellectual refugees, and students arrived to study there from all over Europe; this only made the poor condition in which Bessarion's books were kept even more embarrassing and poignant. Various solutions were proposed, but none was adopted. At first the collection had been kept in a room near the Ducal Palace, and later it was suggested that it be moved to Bon's new building in the Piazza; this came to naught through lack of funds. Fresh impetus to provide a permanent purpose-built library came in the early 1530s through the pressure exerted first by Vettor Grimani (d. 1558), one of the more powerful procurators, and then by Pietro Bembo (1470–1547), who had been appointed librarian and official historian of the Republic.

Sansovino's design for what is now the Biblioteca Nazionale Marciana was formally accepted in 1535, but not begun until two years later. Built of Istrian stone, the façade incorporates a Doric order on the ground floor, with an Ionic *piano nobile* above, then a frieze, and finally a balustrade at the top supporting obelisks and statues of gods and heroes. At first the project advanced slowly, in part because of the difficulty of removing the existing buildings on the site, which included five taverns of dubious reputation, a number of bakeries and the meat market; some of these can be seen in Jacopo de' Barbari's view (see illustration 5) and in a slightly earlier painting

7. The Library, directly opposite the Ducal Palace on the Piazzetta, is a prominent feature of Jacopo Sansovino's scheme. Configured in this way, the two buildings symbolically juxtapose the spaces where justice was dispensed and knowledge obtained.

attributed to Lorenzo Bastiani (see illustration 12). A further setback occurred in late 1545, when the vault of the first bay collapsed. The procurators, holding Sansovino responsible, insisted that the damage (which turned out not to be so dramatic after all) was made good at the architect's own expense, and promptly suspended his salary.

By the 1560s only the first sixteen of the library's twenty-one bays, including the reading room on the first floor, had been finished. The building, which extended as far as the entrance to the Mint, was now in the condition in which Sansovino left it at his death in 1570. A contemporary engraving of the Piazzetta by Jost Amman shows Sansovino's half-finished scheme surrounded by the shops and drinking-holes which still occupied the southern corner of the site. The favourable economic circumstances which had prevailed throughout the 1530s had now given way to more straitened times (inflation was the culprit), but the procurators nevertheless pressed on with the work 'for the honour and dignity of the Republic and for the benefit of the church', conscious that an unfinished building in such a prominent and symbolically significant position was clearly an embarrassment. In the course of the later 1550s efforts were concentrated on the fitting-out and decoration of the interior, presumably in the hope that the library could finally be opened. At an early stage work was begun on the dignified main portal of the reading room, composed of Ionian columns surmounted by a pediment. Shortly afterwards, the ceiling of the reading room, characteristically Venetian in structure, with painted canvasses set into a massive gilded frame, was completed. Seven artists, including Titian and Veronese, the two most prestigious local artists of the day, contributed to the scheme.

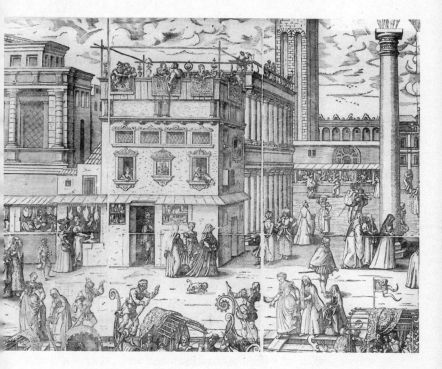

8. This mid-century engraving of the Piazzetta shows Sansovino's scheme still unfinished. Food stalls can be seen in front of the Mint, a tavern occupies the corner site close to the water, and yet more stalls can be seen in the Piazza itself, clustered around the foot of the Campanile.

It was only then that Bessarion's books were finally installed, almost a century after his original bequest had been made.

At the end of the 1550s, with the library still unfinished, the Accademia Venetiana della Fama was briefly given a home in the vestibule (Antisala), which joins the reading room to the staircase leading up to the library from the ground floor. Founded in 1557 by Federico Badoer (1519–93), a diplomat and man of letters, the Venetiana moved there from Badoer's private palace, which had provided a meeting place for what one of its members, in a moment of self-congratulation, called the 'greatest minds' of the city. As a semi-public arrangement, even if not open to all, the academy promoted distinctly Venetian ideas about the value of education and public service in the formation of the Republic's ruling class. With the transference of its seat from Badoer's residence to the Antisala, the links between the Republic and the Venetiana were strengthened. The original intention had been to attract a larger audience for the academy's public lectures, and to collaborate over the arrangement and supervision of Bessarion's collection. Notions of civic duty and pride were to be translated into action. The arrival of the Venetiana helped to underline the concept that the library itself, located within sight of both the Ducal Palace and the Basilica, completed in modern form the material presentation of the core values of the Republic, founded on the ideals of wisdom, Christian belief and now knowledge.

This idea was to be extended further with the almost immediate transformation of the Antisala into a museum of classical antiquities. In 1586, with the interior of the library building complete and the Venetiana now departed, the Senate accepted the gift of an important collection of ancient

9. At the end of the sixteenth century the entrance hall of the library was arranged to accommodate an important collection of antiquities that had been bequeathed to the city. This lent the ensemble a decorous air of antiquity.

marbles from Giovanni Grimani, patriarch of Aquileia. Vincenzo Scamozzi (1548–1616), who had been appointed in 1581 to work up a programme for new housing and offices for the procurators, was given the task of transforming the vestibule of the library into an antiquarium for the display of busts, sculptures and other artifacts from Roman antiquity, with Grimani's bequest in pride of place. Work began in 1591 and, despite difficulties with Grimani's heirs, who refused to permit the removal of a number of reliefs fixed to the walls of the family palace at Santa Maria Formosa, everything was in place by January 1595. The whole scheme had been supervised by Federico Contarini, one of the procurators who was also a dedicated collector of ancient medals, epigraphs, cameos and sculptures; on his death he bequeathed a group of seventeen classical marbles to augment Grimani's collection. Overseen by Titian's ceiling roundel of Sapienza (an allegory of wisdom), the whole ensemble, inventoried and arranged for public display thanks to Contarini's energy and zeal, served as a suitably dignified preface to the library proper. As such it lent a veneer of antiquity which the Venetian past could not provide. In the course of its brief history, Sansovino's building had been library, academy and now museum.

At the southern extremity of the Piazzetta, overlooking the lagoon, stands another vital element of Sansovino's neo-Vitruvian project, the Zecca (Mint). Venice had been minting its own coins since at least the middle of the ninth century, when the inhabitants of the islands of the lagoon first obtained independent trading rights. The workshop which produced them lay close to the Doge's Palace, at the very heart of political power, from at least the end of the tenth century. Sansovino's new building, approved by Doge Gritti and the Council of Ten in 1536, not only replaced the cramped and dangerous conditions of the previous one, which had also been situated on the Molo, it also provided the Republic with an appropriately imposing symbol of its own economic status. Despite being planned immediately after the peace of Bologna of 1529–30, as Venice moved from a policy of militant expansion to a more pacific and politically realistic attitude, Sansovino's building clearly speaks in imperial tones with, unusually, a façade articulated by rustic columns on the ground floor, and a Doric entablature above Tuscan columns on the *piano nobile*. This unconventional approach, in which different classical orders were mixed on a single elevation, was applauded by a number of contemporary architects. Vasari, who knew Sansovino personally, described the Mint as being 'entirely in the most beautiful rusticated order which, never having been seen in the city before, considerably amazed the inhabitants'. The real surprise here, as Sansovino suggests, is not so much the use of rustic columns (even ones so elegant) as their use in a dignified, civic context. Yet further support for the idea came from Sebastiano Serlio (*c.* 1475–*c.* 1554) who, in his treatise on architecture first published in Venice in 1537, pointed out that in ancient Rome the rustic had been freely mixed with Doric, Ionic and Corinthian. The result, he concluded, 'is very attractive to look at, and represents great strength. Thus I would consider it more suitable for a fortress than for anything else.' Sanctioned by both classical precedent and the approval of contemporary practitioners, Sansovino's unusual mixture of orders advertises the building as a place of manufacture, while lending it the dignity appropriate for the storehouse of the state's resources.

By demolishing as well as building, Sansovino heightened

the scenographic theatricality of the project (see page ix). Firstly, by locating the library to the south of the tower he established the boundary of the Procuratie Nuove. Then, with the demolition of the pilgrims' hostel, the Ospizio Orseolo, the west façade of San Marco was fully revealed on the eastern flank of the Piazza. One consequence was that the Campanile, which had previously been somewhat hemmed in by its surrounding buildings, from which it was separated only by narrow alleyways, became even more independent and monumental. These features became more pronounced with the construction of Sansovino's decorative Loggetta (illustration 11). This replaced a plain wooden and stone loggia which had been used by the patricians who came to the Piazza on official business. Some idea of its appearance is provided by the *View of the Piazzetta*, usually attributed to Lorenzo Bastiani (*c.* 1430–1512), which shows a clutch of the nobility grouped around the Pietra del Bando; the façade of the Loggia, a somewhat ramshackle affair, can be clearly seen in the middle foreground, projecting forward from the shops and taverns stretched round the Piazzetta towards the lagoon (see illustration 12). In addition to providing a talking shop for political intrigue, the building had also been used by the procurators for administering the nearby shops and hostelries which lay under their jurisdiction; a seventeenth-century engraving by Giacomo Franco (1556–1620) shows it being used in this way (see illustration 13). In practice there had always been something of a functional separation between the Piazza and the Piazzetta. While the Piazzetta buzzed with political gossip for much of the day, and served on occasion for the processional entry of the doge and distinguished visitors, the Piazza was used

10. Venice minted its own coins in workshops close to the Ducal Palace from at least the thirteenth century. Sansovino's new building for the Mint combines elegance with rustic strength. The central courtyard around which the different workshops were ranged is now roofed over and houses the main reading room of the Biblioteca Marciana.

11. Sansovino's Loggetta, encrusted with marble reliefs and bronze statues, presents a complex of allegorical messages celebrating Venetian achievement. Destroyed when the Campanile collapsed in 1902, it was subsequently reconstructed using fragments of the original.

for state ceremonial which characteristically united civic and religious elements.

The form of the Loggetta is unmistakably derived from the classical triumphal arch. Its façade punctuated by four allegorical bronze statues in niches, and encrusted with a rich programme of densely allusive bas-reliefs in coloured marbles, provides a more dignified, even aulic environment for these activities. Situated at the intersection of the Piazza and the Piazzetta, around which official processions circulated, it was also envisaged as a triumphant celebration of Venetian state ideology. Its iconographical programme was described and explained for the first time by Francesco Sansovino. His authoritative account, published for the first time in 1556 under the pseudonym of Francesco Guisconi and subsequently incorporated into *Venetia città nobilissima*, is a clear example of the role of print in stabilising the interpretation of complex state iconography. In the main panels of the attic storey, Jupiter on Cyprus and Venus on Crete are shown arranged on either side of the figure of Venetia enthroned between two river gods. Taken as a group, these three images allude not only to the origins of the Venetian state, but also to its imperial aspirations and achievements, and to its ability to defend both the territories of the *terraferma* and those of the *terra da mar* against aggressors. The four bronze statues in their niches, which were placed there in 1545, present an allegory of Venetian government. As Sansovino explains, Pallas stands for preparedness, achieved through the sagacity of the Venetian Senate, Mercury represents the eloquence necessary for sound debate and wise decisions, and Apollo, the god of music, provides a symbol of the harmonious society produced by good government. The sequence is completed by Peace, whose special connection with Venice is expressed in the words of Christ to the apostolic protector of the city: '*Pax tibi Marce Evangelista meus*' ('Peace to you, Mark my Evangelist'). A number of the remaining bronze panels which decorate the base of the Loggetta refer to maritime gods, presumably in continuation of the theme of Venetian dominion of the seas announced by the Cyprus and Crete panels in the attic. Perhaps the most decorous of all Sansovino's Venetian buildings, designed in his best Roman manner, the Loggetta was the first public building to be put up in Venice after the peace of Bologna in 1530 and spoke to the imperial theme while at the same time proclaiming patrician control of the square.

With its relentless insistence upon imperial motifs and the virtues of Venetian government, the Loggetta also takes up some of the iconography of the three bronze standard bases designed and executed for the Piazza by Alessandro Leopardi (fl. 1482–1522). These, which stand as a group directly in front of the west façade of the Basilica, support flagpoles from which the standard of Saint Mark, with the Winged Lion picked out in gold thread against a crimson background, was flown on major ceremonial occasions. Commissioned in 1503, they were presumably conceived of as more dignified replacements for the wooden supports for the flagstaffs which can be clearly seen in Bellini's painting (see illustration 1). While the lateral pedestals are identical in their iconography, the central one of the group – the first to be put in place – is decorated with an allegory of Venetian political and economic power expressed through an array of marine animals and goddesses, including Minerva (Peace), Ceres (Abundance) and Astrea (Justice). As Francesco Sansovino recognised, this in effect provides a prologue to the Loggetta itself, and to its principal

12. The Loggia dei Nobili, which Sansovino's Loggetta replaced, can be seen to the right in Lorenzo Bastiani's late fifteenth-century painting of the Piazzetta. In the foreground a group of patricians are gossiping in front of the Pietra del Bando, the low circular column from which official decrees were read out and the heads of traitors displayed.

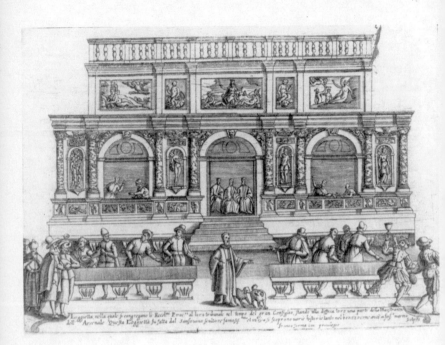

13. The Loggetta being used as a meeting place for the procurators as shown
in an engraving by Giacomo Franco.

message of a benevolent empire, strong both on land and at sea, governed with wisdom and justice. Just as the complex iconography of the Loggetta was explained to a wider public by Francesco in print, so too was that of the standard bases, explained by Pietro Contarini in a poem of 1541.

As the Piazza gradually acquired a more formal and ordered aspect, a last modification was made to Sansovino's Loggetta. The political resonances of the building, with its obvious echoes of the classical triumphal arch and rich sculptural programme, were enhanced by its position in the Piazza itself, the principal arena for official constructions and representations of the state. At some point between Francisco de Holanda's (1517–85) drawing of the completed structure in his Escorial sketchbook, and Giacomo Franco's engraving (which must date from before 1614), the roof of the Loggetta was altered through the addition of a balustrade so as to create a terrace. This may have been done in order to provide a viewing platform from which patricians could observe both the everyday activities in the square and, on ceremonial occasions, the *andata* as it wound its way around the Piazza; the roof of the library was certainly used in this way, while its windows were allocated to the procurators by ballot so that they could watch important events. Women, who were excluded from government and in consequence did not participate in such events, were able to observe from the windows of the first floor of the Procuratie Vecchie – they are shown doing so in Matteo Pagan's *Procession in Saint Mark's Square* (1556–9). By providing an additional vantage point, the functionally enhanced Loggetta emphasised that the real entrance to the Ducal Palace was not, as it is now, from the Piazza and the streets leading into it, but from the lagoon and the Piazzetta.

Both the doge and important visitors who arrived from the water disembarked at the Molo, and then processed between the two columns towards the Loggetta, which is strategically positioned directly opposite the Porta della Carta, the main entrance to the palace. The Scala dei Giganti, which lies beyond, then guided them to the first-floor terrace.

By the time of his death, Sansovino had finished the Loggetta at the foot of the Campanile, sixteen bays of the library facing the Ducal Palace, and the Mint. He had also added the last few remaining bays to the Procuratie Vecchie on the northern side of the Piazza, and had completed the church of San Geminiano, begun by the local architect Cristoforo da Legname in 1505, on the western side. To this small, centrally planned church, Sansovino had been commissioned to add a two-order frontage through the addition of a façade. Similar to one (or perhaps two) of Serlio's projects for temples, published in Book IV of his architectural treatise in 1537, it was demolished along with the church to make way for the Palazzo Reale (Ala Napoleonica) in 1808. Although the library was in use by the time of Sansovino's death in 1570, his design was only finally completed by Vincenzo Scamozzi in the 1580s. In taking up the project, Scamozzi also proposed that an extra storey be added to the library. Although this was rejected, he was able to build to this height with the Procuratie Nuove, which he continued along the south side of the Piazza as far as the church of San Geminiano. In this way Sansovino's original idea of a continuous and stylistically coherent façade running round the square from the library in the Piazzetta to the Torre dell' Orologio was preserved. The scheme was finally completed, though in altered form, by Baldassare Longhena (1598–1682) in the later seventeenth century. After

14. The Piazza and Piazzetta were not only theatrical spaces in themselves, but could also feature on the stage, as in Giacomo Torelli's set for the opera *Bellerofonte*. Displayed for the first time in one of the city's first public opera houses in 1642, it shows the Piazzetta in its traditional guise as the principal entrance to the Piazza.

that, the only significant change to the appearance of the square before the early nineteenth century was the laying of the present pavement, designed by Andrea Tirali in 1722.

In its final form, the configuration of buildings in the Piazzetta turned what had been the most workaday corner of these official spaces into something that was both more formal and more theatrical. Sansovino's use of the different orders on the façades of his new buildings (as if to complement the Doric and Ionic orders deployed on the Mint and the library respectively; the Composite appears on the Loggetta) brings the configuration of all three close in design to the 'Tragic Scene', in one of the illustrations to the second book (1545) of Sebastiano Serlio's architectural treatise. In this way, the Piazzetta carried political meaning as a space not only through traditions of usage as a meeting place for patricians engaged in government business, but also as an appropriate arena, sanctioned by architectural authority and dignified by classical structures, for the activities of the governing class. As Serlio's text explains, the classical and dignified setting, appropriately faced in stone, shown in the 'Tragic Scene', is ideal for noble events, in contrast to the confusion of different styles and materials illustrated in the 'Comic Scene', which Serlio populates with the lower social orders. The idea of the space as a stage is made overt in Giacomo Torelli's 1608–78 design for the set of the Prologue for Francesco Sacrati's opera *Bellorofonte* given its première in Venice in 1642, which consists of a perspectival view of the familiar image of the Piazzetta seen from the lagoon. This is a useful reminder that a vital feature of the life of the square, as it had evolved since the early middle ages, was its role as a theatrical space for the frequent enactment of the rituals of the Republic.

4

RITUAL FORMS

… her daughters had their dowers
From spoils of nations, and the exhaustless East
Pour'd in her lap all gems in sparkling showers:
In purple was she robed, and of her feast
Monarchs partook, and deem their dignity increased.

Lord Byron, *Childe Harold's Pilgrimage*

Early modern Venice was a city of processions. The most visible and elaborate of them, the ducal *andata*, was endlessly reproduced in engravings and woodcuts. Shown in the decorative borders of maps, and described in detail in guidebooks, the experience of the *andata* was one of the strongest impressions of the city that visitors took away with them. The procession itself, which has a long history, is described for the first time by Martin da Canal (around 1275). Among the details familiar from later accounts, Canal notes the presence of a series of symbolic objects known as the *trionfi*, which came to be recognised as emblems of ducal privilege, including the faldstool (a ceremonial folding stool) and six silver trumpets. These, usually referred to as part of the Alexandrine Donation, were given to Doge Sebastiano Ziani by Pope Alexander III (*c.* 1100–81), during a visit to Venice to seek reconciliation with Frederick I Barbarossa as a reward for Ziani's determination both to protect the pope and to intervene in the dispute as a mediator. As Francesco Sansovino explained in the sixteenth century, these ritual gifts, which publicly and symbolically indicated that the doge was the equal of popes and emperors, were triumphantly carried in the ducal procession on all the major occasions in the ceremonial year as both historical relics and emblems of status and authority.

The continuing significance of the Alexandrine Donation in the evolution of the office of doge is commemorated in a set of four canvases painted for the Sala del Maggior Consiglio at the end of the sixteenth century, each of which shows the presentation of a single *trionfo* – candle, sword, umbrella and ring. At the head of the procession in Canal's account, eight standards bearing the Lion of Saint Mark were carried, while at the centre walked the doge, dressed in cloth of gold and wearing his distinctive ceremonial cap (*corno*) decorated with precious stones, preceded by the swordbearer. The second half of the procession included members of the patriciate and important members of the *cittadino* class, the ordinary citizens of Venice.

In a number of significant ways, the *andata* according to Canal is different from that described in later ceremony books. Among the more important is his mention of the '*Laudes Regiae*', an acclamation of the doge, chanted in his honour by the canons of San Marco; like so much else in the civic and religious ceremonials surrounding the figure of the doge, this practice was derived from Byzantium. The chanting of the '*Laudes*' during the investiture of the doge is recorded as early as 1071, but in Venice itself it lapsed during the middle ages. It could be that it was then thought to be an inappropriate glorification of an office which, while it had become increasingly ceremonial in the course of the centuries, was also reduced in power. Matters were different in the colonies. In Dalmatia and Istria, the '*Laudes*' were sung as late as the seventeenth century, presumably as a reminder of Venetian sovereignty exercised through the doge as the representative of Saint Mark on earth.

In its fullest version, as recorded in sixteenth-century texts and images, the *andata* included all the principal office-holders of state together with some minor officials, five foreign ambassadors (representing Rome, Vienna, Madrid, Paris and Constantinople), the canons of the Basilica, the patriarch of Venice (on specified occasions) and, at the core of the procession, the doge himself. By this time the procession had become the most familiar image of the city itself, through its frequent appearance on maps and engravings, mostly produced for pilgrims and tourists. Beginning with Bellini's *Procession*, the *andata* is also occasionally shown in paintings; one of the earliest examples of the genre is Cesare Vecellio's *Procession in Piazza San Marco* (1586), while one of the best known is Canaletto's view of around 1735 showing the arrival of the procession in front of the Scuola di San Rocco. The most detailed visual representation of all is Matteo Pagan's 1556–9 sequence of eight large woodcuts which, when placed in order, present a continuous view of the procession. Pagan's images establish the relative positions of the participants in a way that is confirmed by chronicles and contemporary ceremony books. It has been suggested that, with its three clearly differentiated segments, each arranged in order of precedence, it is possible to interpret the *andata* as a representation of the hierarchical conception of the Republic itself, with its neat

15. Cesare Vecellio's *Procession in Piazza San Marco* of 1586 shows the official procession (*andata*) frozen in a highly idealised and sanitised version of the Piazza.

division into three estates. Although this analysis is probably too schematic (contemporary Venetians were more likely to have recognised individuals rather than offices), the overall organisational principle is clear. The doge was placed at the centre of the procession, the chancery servants of the *cittadino* class were grouped in front and the nobility, who had been elected into the various magistracies, walked behind. Over the course of time, as the question of rank and status as reflected in the ordering of the *andata* became more important, the exact position of each individual office-holder within this structure became more rigidly defined. In all cases, those who walked in the ducal procession did so as the temporary holders of official appointments rather than as individuals in their own right.

On some occasions, the roster of participants was augmented by other social groups, such as the *scuole grandi*, the *scuole piccole*, the trade guilds and sometimes even particular parishes. All the *scuole* crossed neighbourhood boundaries and drew their members from across the city as a whole. Their role in the *andata* had the effect not only of broadening participation in a socially more inclusive way, but of fulfilling political objectives by underlining the allegedly harmonious collective organisation of the city, one of the basic concepts that lay behind the Myth of Venice. Similarly, while the presence of the *scuole* in the procession communicated the idea of communal devotion and charity, the participation of the guilds symbolised the complementary notion of trade as the basis of civic concord. For most Venetian citizens, the most meaningful focus of identity in the sixteenth century was not the *sestiere*, or zone (the city was divided into six), which was merely an administrative unit, but the parish, of which there were about seventy and which, more than any other form of association, generated a sense of local belonging and identity.

On many of the more important feasts in the Venetian calendar, the choir of the San Marco walked in the *andata*. So too, on occasion, did the professional singers employed by some of the wealthier *scuole*. In Bellini's *Procession*, which shows the Scuola di San Giovanni carrying their prized relic of the True Cross on the feast day of Saint Mark, a group of five singers is shown accompanied by an instrumental ensemble. In its expanded form, the *andata* could amplify the liturgy outside the Piazza by processing to other areas of the city as well. On these occasions, civic and liturgical rituals associated with the figure of the doges were enacted outside the central civic and religious arena. This allowed the patrician class not only to broaden the audience for official ceremony, but also to knit together the social fabric of the city through communal ritual acts.

While the *andata* was the most common ritual event to be experienced in the Piazza, by both citizens and foreigners alike, it was not the only one. Rites of passage that marked both the coronation and funeral of the doge were also public occasions, and had been so since the earliest records. The oldest reference to a ducal investiture consisted of just a few lines in John the Deacon's chronicle describing the brief ritualistic moment that marked Doge Pietro Candiano I's formal acceptance of office following his election as doge by popular vote in 887. According to John, Candiano was summoned to the Ducal Palace, where he was presented with three emblems of office – the sword, the baton and the faldstool. In other words, on this occasion the newly elected doge received two of the *trionfi* from the Alexandrine Donation, together with, significantly, the baton of office (*fustis*). This, which is presumably to be equated with the sceptre (*baculus*) mentioned in later medieval accounts of the ceremony, was primarily intended to symbolise the transfer of power to the doge, and to emphasise the continuity of the role. It is notable that Candiano's brief and informal investiture apparently took place in an almost private context (there is no mention of a large crowd of observers), and that it was evidently entirely secular in content.

There is then a gap in the historical documentation of the ceremony until the investiture of Domenico Selvo (d. 1084) at the end of the eleventh century, for which an eyewitness account survives. By this time it had become established practice for the clergy of the city to retreat to the monastery of San Nicolò al Lido, a symbolically significant site since it effectively lies at the confines of the lagoon. There the clergy prayed for divine benediction of the election, wisdom for the electors and a felicitous outcome for all. As in the case of Pietro Candiano I, Selvo's election was by popular assembly according to a set formula of acclaim: '*Domenicum Silvum volumus et laudamus*' ('We want Domenico Selvo and we praise him'). Following this public endorsement he was carried on the shoulders of his supporters to San Nicolò, and then taken by boat across the lagoon to San Marco. During this short trip various songs of praise were sung, together with the '*Te Deum*' and the '*Kyrie Eleison*'. On arrival at the Basilica, Selvo was welcomed by the *primicerio* (the senior ecclesiastic of San Marco), other high-ranking priests and the canons of San Marco. Entering the church barefoot as a sign of humility, Selvo than divested himself of his outer garments, a ritual act that was widely practised throughout the middle ages as part of ceremonies marking the assumption of a new political or ecclesiastical role of elevated status. Next, he prostrated himself in front of the High Altar; the large slab of porphyry in the pavement of the sanctuary may mark the precise spot where this took place. Rising to his feet, Selvo was now presented with the *baculus*, 'as a sign', as one chronicler put it, 'of the conferment of ducal power'. The new doge was then accompanied to the Ducal Palace in solemn procession, where he took an oath of allegiance and distributed gifts to the waiting crowds. It is noticeable that a number of the ceremonial details of Selvo's investiture, clearly expanded from Candiano's ninth-century version, are taken from Byzantium. In Constantinople, the new emperor, greeted with a precise formula, just as Selvo had been at San Nicolò al Lido, was carried on the shoulders of the crowd as a sign of popular acceptance, removed his outer clothing, and then distributed gifts. All these features were still in place at the end of the thirteenth century, when the investiture ceremony was twice described by Martin da Canal.

Many of the details described in Canal's *Les estoires de Venise* are familiar from the few earlier accounts of the ceremony that have survived. These include the election of the doge by popular acclaim, his entry into the Basilica to be formally received by the canons and ecclesiastical dignitaries, the symbolic divestiture, the public oath to protect the heritage of Saint Mark (historically this had always been the primary claim upon the doge), and his triumphant progress through the crowds borne aloft by supporters. By the time that Bartolomeo Bonifacio's detailed ceremony book of the Basilica was being compiled around the middle of the sixteenth century, the choreography of the ducal investiture had become firmly established. Having entered San Marco from the south door leading from the Ducal Palace, the new doge climbed the steps into the *pulpitum magnum* (known popularly as the 'tub'), the large polygonal structure situated to the west of the *iconostasis* (the screen separating the sanctuary from the nave). Constructed of red porphyry sections raised on columns, the pulpit was normally used throughout the middle ages to accommodate the doge on the fairly large number of occasions on which he was required to be present in the Basilica for liturgical and other functions. In terms of its location and use, the *pulpitum magnum* is strongly reminiscent of the way in which the *ambo* functioned in the nave of the Hagia Sophia in Constantinople. This too consisted of a raised platform, supported by columns, located in the southern *exedra*. Also approached by a set of steps, the *ambo* in the Hagia Sophia was used by the emperor when present to hear Mass. The analogies are obviously strong. Moreoever, porphyry had long carried imperial connotations, and its widespread appearance both inside and outside San Marco, and above all in the *pulpitum magnum* itself, implicitly equated the doge with the Byzantine emperor. (Green marble, extensively used both inside and outside San Marco, is appropriate for the ecclesiastical hierarchy as the liturgical colour used for vestments and hangings on ordinary occasions throughout the year. In this way, the dual responsibilities of the building as public space and private chapel of the doge were proclaimed in stone.) It was from this symbolically appropriate place, resonant with a sense of *auctoritas*, that the newly elected doge was presented by the senior elector of the forty-one to the crowds massed in the nave below. The formula used stressed the doge's role as protector of state as well as

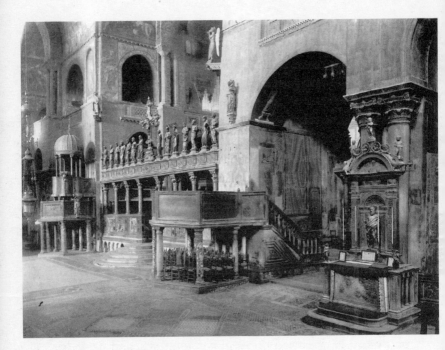

16. Both the screen (*iconostasis*) and the pulpit in San Marco were strongly influenced by Byzantine practice. Sometimes used to seat the doge, for much of the sixteenth century and later the pulpit was used to accommodate the choir of San Marco.

of his own private interests, while the doge's response (again formulaic) promised justice, plenty, peace and the security of the Venetian empire.

From the *pulpitum magnum* the doge now walked to the High Altar, under which lay the relics of Saint Mark in the crypt, and kissed it in a priestly gesture. He was then embraced by the *primicerio*. Both actions, simple enough in themselves, emphasised the semi-sacral character of the dogeship, which is again analogous to that of a Byzantine emperor. During the interval between his election and the investiture ceremonies, the doge was invested with minor orders precisely so that he could legitimately participate in the liturgy, with limited responsibilities (such as the administration of benediction), on a number of specified occasions, particularly during the *triduum* of Holy Week.

Placing his hand on a richly illuminated and ancient copy of the Gospels, the new doge now pledged to protect the patrimony of San Marco. This was a reference not only to the doge's traditional role as the chief custodian of the saint's relics, but also to his responsibility for administering the considerable financial resources of the Basilica, which were bound up in trusts and land holdings. In practice, the daily administration of the business affairs of San Marco was entrusted to the procurators, whose duties also included maintaining a depository for the *specie* of both private individuals and the commune, and also for running a lending bank. As early as the twelfth century this had advanced loans to the government. It was this vital piece of state machinery that the new doge now promised to oversee and protect. Following the taking of this solemn oath, the investiture ceremonies now moved into a new register as they entered their final phase. Taking one of the eight red banners bearing the image of the Lion of Saint Mark from the admiral of the Arsenal, the symbol of Venetian naval power and the source of its trading success and economic wealth, the *primicerio* passed it to the doge saying, 'We consign to your Serenity the banner of Saint Mark as a sign of true and perpetual dogeship', to which he replied, 'I accept.' Originally given to Doge Sebastiano Ziani as part of the Alexandrine Donation, and hence one of the *trionfi*, the banners were an image of ducal status and authority, and as such were carried at the head of the *andata* on important ceremonial occasions. Kept in the Arsenal, they could be one of four different colours according to the current condition of Venetian diplomatic and military affairs: white stood for peace, red for war, blue signified attachment to an alliance, and violet indicated a state of truce. Their reappearance at this critical moment in the investiture marks the symbolic transference of power into the hands of the new doge. Introduced into the ceremony in the course of the twelfth century, the presentation of the banner of Saint Mark, symbol of the *commune veneciarum*, replaced that of the sceptre, which was probably abandoned because of its monarchical overtones. Of equal significance was a further change made to the investiture ceremony at about the same time, through the addition of an oath of office that limited ducal power.

This solemn moment, when the new doge was effectively consecrated, appeared on Venetian coinage. Carried in pouches, and exchanged over tables and in shops, this familiar image served as a constant reminder to the Venetians of the central politico-theological concept of the elected head of state as Saint Mark's representative on earth, and as the principal mediator on behalf of its citizens in times of crisis. By the sixteenth century, this central episode of the investiture was marked by the singing of the *Oration di San Marco*, of which settings survive by a number of the most distinguished Venetian composers:

O Lord who has exalted your Evangelist, blessed Mark, because of his preaching of the gospel, we implore you, grant that we may always be assisted by his teaching and protected by his prayers. Alleluia.

During the early middle ages, and as late as the fifteenth century, the presentation of the sceptre, a clear indicator of kingship, was amplified by the singing of the '*Laudes Regiae*'. This is a sequence of acclamations whose origins can be traced back to classical times, and which was later incorporated into both imperial and papal ceremonial. As with so many details of the ceremonies surrounding the doge, the more immediate model was again probably Byzantium, where the '*Laudes*' were also sung to enhance the splendour of the emperor and his court.

It is highly suggestive that the only polyphonic (musical) setting of the Venetian '*Laudes Regiae*' was composed in honour of Francesco Foscari in the first half of the fifteenth century. His dogeship, at thirty-four years the longest in the history of the Republic, is notable for the way in which the powers of the office were extended at a time when the conquest of the towns of the *terraferma* had been completed and the Venetian state was at the height of its imperial ambitions. This was also a period when, to many observers, Venice appeared to be in pursuit of the control of northern Italy, provoking criticism from those who believed such a policy to be a mistake, a diversion from the maritime trade on which the city's greatness had been founded, and one which could only provoke the enmity of its Italian neighbours as well as foreign powers. Eventually these fears were to become reality with the formation of the League of Cambrai, whose forces disastrously routed Venetian troops at the battle of Agnadello in 1509. But in the heyday of empire, when the new Venetian territories on the mainland were being consolidated, the grandiloquent aspirations of many patricians found expression in grandiose architectural projects of all kinds. Foscari himself led the way, within just one year of his election as doge, with the construction of Ca' Foscari, the most imposing private palace ever to be built on the Grand Canal, and a clear challenge in terms of elegance, grandeur and sheer size to Ca' d'Oro, where building had been begun three decades earlier. In the Piazza San Marco, it was Foscari who promoted the continuation of the Piazzetta wing of the Ducal Palace in the direction of the Basilica. The original fourteenth-century building had terminated at the seventh portico, with Calendario's roundel encapsulating the statue of Venecia/Justice above; this was now continued towards the Basilica, using the same building materials and the same distinctive geometrical design as the lagoon façade, to reach a magisterial conclusion with the Porta della Carta, so-called because of its proximity to the archive of official government records. It was also Foscari who commissioned the Arco Foscari, an elaborate gateway flanked by statues of the virtues of Temperance, Fortitude, Prudence and Charity (all considered to be essential for good governance), and crowned by a delicate arched window of florid gothic tracery. Immediately above the entrance is a statue of Foscari himself kneeling before the Lion of Saint Mark, while at the apex of the structure sits (again) the figure of Venetia/ Justice enthroned. There could hardly be a more evocative image of the total identification, for political purposes, of a single individual with the office of doge. With the exception of Andrea Gritti in the sixteenth century, no other doge made such a decisive impact on the visual appearance of the square.

The self-aggrandising tendencies of Foscari's dogeship form part of a recurrent cycle characterised by periods of authoritarian behaviour exercised by strong-willed doges followed by periods of restraint. Among Foscari's successors as powerful and determined holders of the post were Agostino Barbarigo (*c.* 1420–1501) and, in particular, Andrea Gritti (1456–1538). Leaving aside such prominent examples of firm rule and masterful behaviour, the overall tendency over time was for ducal power to be diminished. This had the effect of restricting the scope for individual initiative, and spreading the power base rather than allowing influence to accumulate in the hands of a single family. In reality, however, those elected to the dogeship came from a small, select group taken from the rollcall of patrician families whose names were recorded in the *Libro d'oro*, since only a few were of sufficient means to support the lifestyle associated with the office. And, in a historical paradox familiar from other contexts (Edwardian Britain and its empire provides an analogous example), the ceremonials and rituals surrounding the head of state only increased in complexity as the power of the office itself diminished. The doge had to be respected and obeyed, at least in minor matters, but in questions of greater importance he was impotent without support. It was presumably this notion of the constraints of power that the diarist Girolamo Priuli had in mind when he wrote:

It is commonly said that a Venetian prince is a mere tavern sign and that he cannot do anything without the agreement of his councillors, the Collegio, or the councils. But I want to emphasise that a Venetian prince may do as he wants. Everyone seeks his goodwill and tries to be agreeable to him, and if occasionally there is a councillor or someone else who wants to oppose him, it is best to proceed with caution, otherwise he will meet a severe rebuff and embarrassment. It is true that if a doge does anything against the Republic he won't be tolerated, but in everything else, even small matters, he does as he pleases as long as he doesn't offend the honour and dignity of the state.

Questions of honour and dignity were much in evidence during the ceremonies that articulated the last three days of Holy Week, culminating in Easter Sunday, when the doge was one of the central actors in the rituals that took place both in the Basilica and outside in the Piazza. During the early middle ages (the practice was later discontinued), he also performed the *mandatum*; this involved washing the feet of twelve pre-selected male citizens during the Maundy Thursday ceremonies, a gesture which symbolically equated the doge with Christ, who washed the feet of the Apostles on the day before the Crucifixion.

The semi-sacral nature of the office again came into play during the funeral rites which followed the death of the doge, rites which (in common with the investiture) were to a considerable extent conducted in public. The death itself was announced to the population at large by the ringing of nine peals of doubles from the Campanile in the Piazza; the same change was then taken up by all the churches and monasteries of the city. The extraordinary cacophony that must have resulted also served the practical purpose of summoning all members of the Great Council to the Ducal Palace to begin the process of electing a successor. Continuity was of the essence, and the seamless transition (as it was hoped) from one doge to the next was indicated by the speed with which the process was begun. Almost immediately, three contingents of shipbuilders (known as *arsenalotti*) were despatched from the Arsenal to safeguard the Ducal Palace. In part this was a relic of earlier, more disordered times, when the doge's apartments were routinely pillaged by the crowds gathered in the Piazza following the announcement of his death. Even in the sixteenth century unrest was not unknown. During the election of 1559, which finally settled on Girolamo Priuli, it emerged that there was a strong body of support for Girolamo Grimani, who was strongly disliked by ordinary Venetians. The crowds who had gathered in the Piazza to express their displeasure began to beat on the doors of the Ducal Palace chanting, 'If you elect Grimani we will throw him to the dogs!' During the election of Alvise Mocenigo in 1570, it was forbidden to carry weapons in the Piazza; unruly bands of soldiers, recruited for the war against the Turks, were on the loose, and violence was feared.

Behind closed doors, hidden from public gaze, the body of the deceased doge was solemnly stripped of his symbols of office. First his gold ring was handed to one of the secretaries of the Council of Ten, who smashed it to pieces. Next followed the matrix from which the doge's seal was made for official documents. This too was destroyed. Finally, two silver vessels from the salt works at Chioggia were produced. Situated at the southern extremity of the lagoon, Chioggia's history had always been intimately linked with that of Venice, and the salt works, which proved a considerable source of income, was established there in the twelfth century. The larger of the two vessels, decorated with the familiar image of the doge holding the banner of Saint Mark, was shattered, while the smaller one was taken away to be engraved with the name of the new doge once the result of the election was known. These actions emphasised both the end of a doge's personal authority and the continuity of his office. Much the same message was transmitted by the rituals that took place later the same day. Then, solemnly dressed in cloth of gold, the corpse of the dead doge was carried from his private apartments in the Ducal Palace to the Sala dei Pioveghi; there it was laid out on a catafalque which was also draped in cloth of gold. Here the ducal crown was removed from the body and placed on the faldstool. Another ritual object from the Alexandrine Donation, the gold ceremonial sword, was displayed pointing downwards, while reversed spurs were attached to the doge's feet. Accompanying the body were twenty patricians dressed in red (known as the *scarlatti*); their presence signified the continuity of republican government during the interval between one doge and the next, while the festal colours of their robes were meant 'as a sign', as the diarist Marin Sanudo put it, 'that the Signoria still lives though the doge is dead'. For three days and nights the corpse lay in solemn state, while groups of *scarlatti* took it in turn to keep watch, and requiems for the soul of the deceased were sung in the Basilica. At the end of this period the obsequies gradually moved from the private to the public sphere. As so often with Venetian ceremonial, this was achieved through processional forms which, in this case, symbolically retraced the route taken by the doge following his investiture in San Marco.

The day began with the Office of the Dead chanted

around the catafalque in the presence of the papal legate and the foreign ambassadors. Accompanied by the entire Senate, the body was now carried to the head of the Scala dei Giganti – that is, to precisely the place where the doge had publicly taken the oath of office and had received the *corno* during his investiture. At this juncture the senators returned to the Ducal Palace, where they were to participate in the election of the new doge; their absence from the funeral procession itself further underlined the concept of continuity. For all intents and purposes the deceased doge, as he now left the palace and was carried into the Piazza for the last time, reverted from being the temporary holder of the highest office of state to the condition of a private person.

The long funeral cortège which now wound its way round Saint Mark's Square behind the corpse included monks and nuns from the monasteries of the city, representatives of the *scuole piccoli*, the nine clerical orders, and members of the doge's family. The six *scuole grandi* also walked in the procession, with pride of place immediately behind the open coffin being reserved for the members of the *scuola* to which the doge had belonged. The cortège having arrived in front of the Basilica, the corpse was raised in the air nine times, while the cry went up, 'God have mercy!' and nine doubles rang out from the Campanile.

Beginning with Domenico Selvo, elected in 1071, most of the early doges were buried inside San Marco. This may well have been in recognition of the contribution that they had made to the construction and decoration of the Contarini church, though again there is also a possible connection with Byzantine practice, which may have provided a model for the Venetians, since the Apostoleion in Constantinople, together with the contiguous mausoleum of Constantine the Great, had served as the favoured final resting place of the emperors. In Venice, the erection of Andrea Dandolo's tomb in the Baptistery of the Basilica in 1354 put a stop to the tradition of interring the doges inside San Marco. The reasons for this are unclear, but it may be that the flamboyant design of Dandolo's tomb chest alarmed those patricians ever-suspicious of monarchical or imperial tendencies in the behaviour of individual doges; certainly Dandolo's precedent, in terms of both style and location, would have had the effect of turning San Marco into a mausoleum had it been followed by his successors. Thereafter doges were buried in one of the city churches, with the Franciscan church of the Frari and the Domenican one of Santi Giovanni e Paolo, the two great mendicant churches of Venice, being the preferred sites. Leonardo Loredan (1436–1521) is among those buried in the latter and Francesco Foscari in the former, while Andrea Gritti's tomb is in the church of San Francesco della Vigna, designed by his friend Jacopo Sansovino and begun during his dogeship. Examples of powerful and autocratic doges, all these men were none the less laid to rest well away from the Piazza and its surrounding official buildings which had served as a theatre for so much of their public actions and greatest triumphs during their years in office.

Frozen in space and time in engravings and paintings, such official ceremonies of state have helped to consolidate the sense of the Piazza as a purely formal forecourt to the Basilica and the Ducal Palace. Reading the ceremony books and contemplating the evidence of images such as Vecellio's *Procession* only serve to heighten the impression of the square as an ordered and official space, a parade ground for carefully choreographed symbolic state rituals. In part this was its function, but at the same time the Piazza was also the site of more mundane activities, from baking bread to selling sex.

5

. . . .

URBAN NOISE

Here is the greatest magnificence of architecture to be seene, that
any place under the sunne doth yeelde. Here you may both see
all manner of fashions of attire, and heare all the languages of
Christendome, besides those that are spoken by the barbarous
Ethnickes; the frequencie of people being so great twise a day,
betwixt sixe of the clocke in the morning and eleven, and againe
betwixt five in the afternoon and eight, that a man may very
properly call it rather Orbis *than* Urbis *forum, that is, a market*
place of the world.

Thomas Coryate, Coryat's Crudities

As well as being the arena for dignified official spectacles, the
Piazza also reverberated to the sounds of less austere activities. These ranged from the buying and selling of produce to
the exhortations of charlatans and quacks, the performances
of street entertainers and the cries of hawkers and pedlars.
Carefully erased from official images and descriptions of the
square, they can be reinstated thanks to the observations of
foreign visitors and from the records of court proceedings
when the procurators moved against lawbreakers and trans-
gressors. Particularly rich in detail from this point of view
is the voluminous and rambling diary kept from January

1496 until June 1533 by Marin Sanudo, some 40,000 pages bound up into fifty-eight volumes now housed in the State Archives in Venice. As a source of information of all kinds it is without parallel. In order to compile it Sanudo went to the Ducal Palace virtually every day for almost forty years, bringing back with him accounts of elections and debates, digests of official documents, copies of private letters, transcripts of new reports from abroad and eyewitness descriptions of daily life in the city. To these, carefully copied into his diary, he sometimes added bits of printed ephemera, testimony to the growing importance of print culture as a source of information about current events. As with all such compilations, the value of Sanudo's diary varies enormously according to the material presented. Conscious from the first that it was not a secret and private affair (it was conceived as a sort of database for the monumental history of Venice that Sanudo intended to write but never did), events that he considered to be an embarrassment to the government were often suppressed. Ever hopeful of being appointed to the prestigious post of official historian to the Republic, Sanudo was a good company man. But as an observer of the minutiae of everyday existence in Renaissance Venice he is unbeatable. It is from Sanudo that we learn of the climate, the elections of doges, prices in the markets at Rialto and naval manoeuvres of the Venetian galleys in the Adriatic. And it is also from Sanudo that we hear about life in Piazza San Marco in all its many guises, whether as official processional space, the site of the annual Ascension Day fair, the embarkation point for pilgrims bound for the Holy Land or a bustling marketplace full of taverns and food stalls. Without Sanudo it would be hard to put the life, noise and smell of the Piazza back into our imaginative recreations of how it was in that distant past, scrubbed clean of such details as it has been by official accounts.

Among the more riotous of the annual events staged in the square was the celebration of Giovedì Grasso, the last Thursday of carnival (which ends on Shrove Tuesday), when a number of pigs and a bull were released into the Piazzetta. There they were remorselessly chased and captured. There followed a mock trial, at the end of which the animals were condemned to death by the Magistrato del Proprio, one of the highest legal officers of state. Once sentence had been delivered, the pigs were handed over to members of the blacksmiths' and butchers' guilds for their meat to be cut up and distributed to the crowd. This gruesome spectacle was watched by the doge, members of the Signoria and the foreign ambassadors, as well as a large and unruly public. The origins of this cruel and bizarre performance lay in the twelfth century, when, in the course of one of the periodic disputes over ecclesiastical jurisdiction which characterised relations between Venice and Aquileia, the patriarch of Aquileia was taken hostage. After some negotiation he was released, but only on condition that a tribute (in effect a gesture of submission) be sent to Venice each year so as to arrive in time for Giovedì Grasso. The tribute consisted of a bull (to represent the patriarch) and twelve pigs (in recollection of the twelve Friulian lords who supported his cause), together with twelve loaves of bread.

Once the carnage was over, the doge and Signoria, dressed in ceremonial scarlet (which was otherwise worn only on Palm Sunday and Christmas Day), retreated to the Ducal Palace, where they smashed small wooden models of castles

17. Pigs being butchered in the Piazzetta on the last Thursday of carnival. Traditionally held in front of a large crowd, this gruesome event was also watched by the doge and other officers of the state. Giacomo Franco's engraving of the spectacle helps to modify the traditional image of the space as purely ceremonial.

in commemoration of the Venetian victory. Although Aquileia had ceased to be an autonomous territory in the early fifteenth century, the Venetian authorities continued to stage this popular part of the carnival season despite its irrelevance as a political act. During the sixteenth century there were a number of attempts to abolish it. In 1525 the Council of Ten, as part of a more general reform of carnival itself, attempted in vain to limit the brutality; Sanudo reports that animals were slaughtered the following year. According to Francesco Sansovino, it was largely through the influence of Doge Andrea Gritti, motivated by a complex of moral, political and aesthetic reasons, that efforts were made to contain the savagery as part of an initiative to shift the Venetian carnival into a more elevated mode. This sometimes involved introducing learned elements thought to be more in keeping with the increasingly dignified appearance of the Piazza as it began to be transformed. In 1532, an allegorical procession was staged in the Piazza on Giovedì Grasso; this was followed by a mock battle in which the Vices were defeated by the Virtues, and the Temple of Peace was revealed. By way of conclusion, the victors celebrated with a boisterous dance. This simple allegorical presentation, characteristic of the distancing from popular traditions which Gritti and his supporters attempted to introduce, has also been seen as characteristic of a more general trend towards the cultural separation of social classes that was typical of the last half of the sixteenth century. In this process, pressure for a more decorous outcome was exercised through an emphasis on a classical vocabulary in much official art and architecture, and in increasingly elaborate state spectacle.

Fresh pork, especially that produced in such a bizarre and

bloodthirsty way, was not the only food to be found there. Since the early middle ages, a wide variety of produce had been sold in the Piazza, the Piazzetta and the surrounding areas. There were markets for meat and fish, and next to the Mint stood the huge gothic granaries of the Republic. Early descriptions of the area mention shops selling cheese and salami and taverns strung out along the Molo and round the corner into the Piazzetta, while directly in front of the west front of the Basilica were meat and vegetable stalls. Clustered around the two columns at the entrance to the Piazzetta from the lagoon stood further booths. Shops and taverns along the waterside are also mentioned by Marcantonio Sabellico in his history of Venice. Some of these structures can be seen quite clearly in Jacopo de' Barbari's bird's-eye view and in Bastiani's *View of the Piazzetta*. (See illustrations 5 and 12.)

Once Sansovino's plans for the redevelopment of the Piazza had been adopted by the procurators, it became necessary to clear away some of these eyesores. In theory this should have been comparatively easy, since most of the premises were owned by the procurators themselves, but in practice matters were more complicated. Rental income from the various shops and stalls was considerable, and in the battle between aesthetics and Mammon the latter frequently triumphed. Some of the tenants had longstanding rights which they refused to relinquish and, since much of the trade catered for the large numbers of foreign visitors and pilgrims who gathered in the square, it was impractical to remove taverns, guesthouses and money-changing activities without finding alternative sites. Throughout the sixteenth century and beyond, as Sansovino's grand scheme slowly reached completion, frequent attempts were made by the authorities to clean up the Piazza. On one occasion it was even suggested that all commercial activity be removed except during the annual fair that took place around the feast of the Ascension (the Sensa). In practice little was achieved. In 1529 the space around the columns was cleared and eight new stalls were provided along the waterfront beyond the Mint for the uprooted fruit and vegetable sellers but when, at the end of the decade, the bread shops on the library site were demolished, the bakers were simply rehabilitated at the foot of the columns where the greengrocers had been. There they remained for a further ten years until they too were relocated at the base of the Campanile. Although this was not thought to be an ideal solution, the bakeries remained there until they were destroyed in the fire of 1574; even then they were simply rebuilt in the same place. In addition to these legal traders there were also illegal ones, most of whom sold eggs, poultry, fruit and vegetables. For many of these business was so lucrative that they easily could afford the penalty and confiscation of goods that the procurators periodically imposed until, in some desperation, the Council of Ten produced a decree banning all stalls from around the columns and under the arcades of the Ducal Palace. In 1531, the five shops owned by the procurators on the Ponte della Pescaria were being rented to a glazier, a cheesemonger, a fruiterer and two poulterers; they can still be seen there, together with the fish market, in eighteenth-century views. So too can the stalls in the northeast corner of the Piazza, clustered at the foot of the Torre dell' Orologio and around Leopardi's standard bases in front of the Basilica. In addition, according to an ancient right granted at the end of the fourteenth century, sellers of jewellery and trinkets were allowed to operate in the Piazza on market days. Opposition was occasionally mounted by the guilds, but the right was upheld and the trade continued.

More sombre activities also took place there, since those convicted of crimes both minor and major were brought to the Piazzetta with some regularity to be punished in full view of a curious public. During his visit, Coryate witnessed the 'very Tragicall and doleful spectacle' of two men being tortured with the strappado. On such occasions this part of the square became the arena for the enforcement of the subliminal message that the Republic was an ordered state where violence was controlled, evil was not tolerated and crime was countered with just retribution. The site between the two columns was symbolically ideal for these purposes; there the guilty were overseen not only by Theodore and Mark, the two patron saints of the city, but also by the nearby images of Venecia/Justice on the façades of the Ducal Palace.

Appropriate though the site was, the reasons for its choice may have been more prosaic. According to legend, when the two columns arrived in Venice, Doge Sebastiano Ziani promised a reward to anyone who could safely lift them into place. The prize was claimed by one Nicolò il Barattiere, who demanded that he should be allowed to set up public gaming tables between the two pillars as his prize. Although Ziani could not go back on his promise, it was decided that the public executions which previously had taken place near San Giovanni in Bragora should be moved here so that it became tainted as a place of ill omen. None the less, business continued to be conducted between the columns.

In more serious criminal cases, those convicted were dragged from one part of the city to another by horse before being brought to the Piazzetta for execution, which was then carried out on a temporary platform so that the crowds could obtain a good view. Accompanying the guilty was a priest and the hooded members of the Scuola di San Fantin, a confraternity dedicated to the charitable task of assisting prisoners on their last journey. As they moved slowly in procession, members of the Scuola rattled their chains to announce the impending spectacle. In the case of thieves, this was merely the finale of a much longer and more painful process in which the convicted were taken back to the scene of their crime before having their hands cut off and hung around their necks; in this sorry condition they were then taken to the Piazza to be despatched. The official rhetoric which accompanied these public displays of justice in action evidently worked. Writing to Andrea Gritti in 1530, the poet Pietro Aretino (1492–1556) praised Venice as both a haven of freedom and a model of the well-ordered state free of crime:

> *Here treachery has no place, here reigns neither the cruelty of harlots nor the insolence of the effeminate, here there is no theft, or violence, or murder … O universal homeland! Custodian of the liberties of man! Refuge of exiles!*

These final exclamations, with their resonances of Petrarch, are commonplace enough. As for the rest, it would be interesting to know what precisely Aretino thought he was doing. It seems highly unlikely that, having collaborated with the engraver Marcantonio Raimondi (*c.* 1480–*c.* 1534) to produce the most pornographic illustrated book of the entire Italian Renaissance, he would not have noticed the army of whores to be found in every *sestiere* of the city, some of them whispering their entreaties under the arcades of the Piazza.

In addition to cures for the body, sustenance for the mind was on offer. Single-sheet broadsides, engravings and pamphlets were hawked by itinerant sellers around the Basilica or under the arcades in the square. It is again Pietro Aretino who gives a lively impression of the trade in 'Pretty tales, tales, tales, the Turkish war in Hungary, Father Martin's sermons, the Council, tales, tales, the facts of England, the festivities of the Pope and the Emperor, the circumcision of the Voivoda, the Sack of Rome, the Siege of Florence, the battle at Marseilles and its conclusion, tales, tales ...' Many of these stories came out of tradition – romances and chivalric tales were always popular – but, as Aretino suggests, news of foreign parts, and above all wars, was also of interest. Strolling players, actors and buffoons were a common sight in the open spaces of Venice, and nowhere more so than in the Piazza. Here outdoor performers would set out benches to stand on, or put up temporary staging. Once the crowds had gathered, they would be entertained with epic tales or accounts of current events, sung to simple melodic formulas arranged in short verses. The texts themselves were sometimes printed in crudely produced pamphlets of a few pages, to be sold to the audience as souvenirs; Sanudo describes one actor who hawked copies of his monologues immediately after the performance. Ludovico Ariosto's epic poem *Orlando Furioso* (1516), a great favourite, was available in severely truncated 'popular' versions which isolated key moments in the story, printed in old-fashioned and worn gothic type in octavo or even smaller formats. These too were texts to be sung, and could touch all levels of society; one sixteenth-century writer claimed that he had seen *Orlando* 'read by the old, read by the young, cherished by men, valued by women, prized by the learned, sung by the ignorant, possessed by all in the cities, and taken with them to the country'. *Orlando* and other chivalric stories apart, news from abroad was staple fare, not surprisingly in a city whose inhabitants were often engaged in war, above all with the Turks.

In addition to the songs of the strolling players, the Piazza also resounded to the blandishments of the charlatans and mountebanks who used music as part of their pitch. Some were properly qualified doctors and professional toothpullers; for them music not only attracted attention and brought in business, but was thought to bring relief from pain and formed part of the healing process. Others were simply quacks and frauds. Coryate saw five or six groups of mountebanks working from raised stages, while others operated from the pavement of the square. These groups, which appeared in both the morning and the afternoon, included both men and women. The proceedings began with music – sometimes vocal, sometimes instrumental, occasionally both – followed by a preamble which began the sales pitch. At this point a trunk, which had been dragged up on to the stage, was thrown open to reveal 'a world of new-fangled trumperies'. The value and miraculous properties of these wares were then extolled at length, perhaps for as long as an hour, in order to wear down the resistance of bystanders. Although these activities attracted the attention of the authorities from time to time, attempts at regulation never succeeded for long, and charlatans and mountebanks continued to be a feature of the square, cajoling and swindling their audiences, until the end of the Republic in 1797. They, along with much else, were to be swept away by Napoleon Bonaparte.

In addition to the locals, the Piazza was also a meeting place for foreigners of all kinds, in particular pilgrims. Throughout the middle ages the pilgrimage was a reasonably common experience, part of a complex of religious phenomena that included cults of the saints, indulgences, relics and miracles. At the same time it was also an adventure of a particularly ambitious kind, since the indulgences obtained in the course of the journey represented a major investment in salvation itself. For European Christians the most important pilgrimage that could be made was to the Holy Land. It was also the most dangerous, and many lives were lost through disease, shipwrecks and the depredations of pirates. Eberhard, count of Württemberg, claimed that there were three things in life which could be neither encouraged nor deprecated: marriage, war and the journey to the Holy Sepulchre. All might begin well, but could end badly.

In 1486 Bernhard von Breydenbach (1440–97), dean of Mainz cathedral, published an account of his pilgrimage to visit the holy places, made a few years earlier together with a number of companions. Issued in a handsome edition enlivened with a number of fold-out city views, Breydenbach's book is the most elegant of what was to become a distinct genre of travel literature. With three editions in Latin, three in French, three in German and one each in Flemish and Spanish, all of which appeared within a short span of time, it also became one of the most widely known. Perhaps the most familiar of all the views in Breydenbach's book is a woodcut of Venice, on four sheets glued together, which is accompanied by a brief historical description of the city. Together with more popular (and less expensive) guides such as Noè Bianchi's frequently reprinted *Viazo da Venesia*, written following his pilgrimage of 1446–50, such books not only added

18. Erhard Reuwich's *View of Venice* from Bernhard von Breydenbach's
Peregrinatio in Terram Sanctam of 1486, the first printed travel book. In it
Breydenbach gives an account of his pilgrimage to the Holy Land. The book
also contains the earliest detailed printed view of Venice, incorporated as a
fold-out illustration, with the Piazzetta clearly shown.

to the fame of Venice abroad but in some cases also created a mental picture of its principal monuments for those who never went there. From early in its history, the illustrated printed book stimulated armchair travel, and in the process imaginatively created striking visual images of the Piazza.

Italians flocked to Venice to set out on this great spiritual journey, but so too did pilgrims from northern Europe, particularly the English, French, Dutch and Germans. It is no surprise that so many personal accounts of such a fundamental experience survive, copied into diaries and commonplace books. Many records of such an important and hazardous experience became family icons, passed on with care and admiration from one generation to another. At a basic level many of them are simple, practical compilations, full of useful jottings about food, monuments to be visited, the distances between them, the employment of guides, the weather, indulgences to be sought and the prices of everything. Others move more in the direction of genuine personal observation and give not only some impression of the author's self, but also occasional glimpses of Venice as seen through the eyes of an outsider. While many rehearse the standard 'wonders of Venice', often in almost identical wide-eyed rhetorical terms, there are occasional surprises. One fifteenth-century pilgrim, Felix Fabri, found the city to be full of the nobility 'from every region of the world, gathered to make the trip across the sea to visit the Holy Sepulchre', a useful corrective to the conventional image of the impoverished barefoot pilgrim. Another, the Dutch pilgrim Arendt Willemsz, provides invaluable information, not to be gained from any other historical source, about liturgical ceremonies (and their music) in the early sixteenth century.

By the end of the fifteenth century Venice controlled most of the pilgrimage trade to the Holy Land. In earlier times the trip could be made from a number of ports around the Mediterranean – in particular, Ancona, Genoa, Pisa, Montpellier and Marseilles – but in the end it was only the Venetians who could provide a reasonably safe passage across the Mediterranean to Jaffa. A measure of protection against attacks from Barbary pirates was provided by the Republic's galleys, while Venetian trading posts and harbours along the Istrian and Dalmatian coasts, and on Cyprus and Crete, formed a string of safe havens along the route. Before setting out on the journey, pilgrims normally stayed in Venice for some weeks, usually in one of the hostels devoted to the purpose (with each 'nation' having its own), in order to make all the necessary arrangements: money had to be changed, prices and conditions agreed with the ship's master and provisions laid in. Specialised guides, the *tolomazi*, were to be found lurking around the money-changers' booths at the foot of the Campanile, offering to help with these negotiations in return for a fee; their reputation for sharp practice, made all the easier by language difficulties, was legendary. The pilgrimage trade must have been a significant part of the commercial activities in and around the Piazza, particularly as spring approached and the galleys were repaired and readied for departure on the new tides.

So too must have been the associated activities of indulgence-gathering and relic-hunting. In the weeks of waiting for the voyage to begin, spiritual preparations could be made by visiting important devotional sites in Venice itself. The city was home to one of the richest collections of relics anywhere in the Christian world outside Rome, including, allegedly, the body of Saint Lucy, the head of Saint George and part of the sponge used by the centurion at the Crucifixion. Churches and convents where these remains were displayed formed part of a devotional topography which connected some of the more outlying areas of Venice with the central focus of the Piazza, where the Basilica housed the most prestigious relic of all, the remains of Saint Mark. Pilgrims snaked along these routes, singing and praying as they went, in search of indulgences. Those from northern Europe had begun their devotional accounting much further afield. A group of pilgrims from Delft who set out for Venice en route to the Holy Land in 1525 stopped in Maastricht, where they were shown the head of Saint Mary Magdalene and a fragment of Noah's Ark, and Cologne, where the remains of Saint Ursula and the heads of the Three Magi were venerated. From here they took to the Rhine, and then crossed the Alps and descended to Venice, where they arrived at Whitsuntide and took rooms at the White Lion, a traditional haunt of German and Dutch visitors. Jacques Le Saige, a silk merchant from Douai who made the pilgrimage to Jerusalem in 1518 together with four companions, prefaced the voyage with a long stay in Rome specifically to visit relics and collect indulgences. In the context of such journeys, arrival in the Holy Land was the culmination of a much more ambitious undertaking in which Venice, and above all the Piazza, played a fundamental role. On the feast of Corpus Christi, on the Thursday after Trinity Sunday, those soon to embark for Jerusalem were incorporated into a vast procession which was, in effect, an expanded form of the ducal *andata*. Once again, the Piazza became the site of a great spectacle which united different elements of the wider Venetian community, in this case the permanent and the temporary. Some impression of this crowded occasion (thousands must have participated) is provided by an early seventeenth-century engraving by Giacomo Franco.

One fifteenth-century English pilgrim, Sir Richard Guylforde, records his experience of the event, noting that the pilgrims processed 'with lyghte in our hands of wexe, of the freshest formynge, geven unto us by the mynysters of the sayde procession'. The power of this unassuming ritual gesture was considerable, since the symbolic meaning of candles, common enough throughout Catholic Europe, carried a quite precise set of meanings in Venice. Frequently carried by members of the confraternities, both processionally on special occasions and as they went about their daily business, candles assumed a particular significance in relation to the cult of Saint Mark. On the vigil of his feast day, a vespers procession which included the *trionfi* walked around the square and then entered the Basilica where, during the singing of the Magnificat, the doge lit a candle in honour of the Evangelist and placed it on the High Altar. Behind this simple act, which annually renewed the links between Mark and the city, lay the Alexandrine Donation, when the pope had presented the doge with a candle in recognition of this special relationship; the Donation and its significance was recalled in turn on every occasion that the *andata* took place, through the presence of a white candle placed in a strategic position directly in front of a page bearing the ducal *corno* on a ceremonial cushion. In this context, the presentation of candles to the pilgrims walking in the Corpus Christi procession by the senators who accompanied them took on a greater significance, intensified since the candles themselves were preserved and carried to Jerusalem to be placed in front of the Holy Sepulchre.

19. On the feast of Corpus Christi pilgrims from all over Europe walked in procession in the Piazza. Shown here in an engraving by Giacomo Franco, the occasion provided a Venetian benediction for great spiritual enterprise. By the sixteenth century Venice was virtually alone in being able to provide a safe passage to the Holy Land.

In later centuries, when the Venetian pilgrimage trade had dwindled to virtually nothing, each senator in the procession was accompanied by a member of the Venetian poor, who was presented with clothing, money and a candle, the latter gift being a remnant of the historic practice. This process is characteristic of much ritual of the Republic, transforming the universally Christian into the specifically Venetian by appropriating a common festal act celebrated throughout Catholic Europe and investing it with local significance. In this way Venice became a psychological and symbolic extension of the sacred space of Jerusalem itself, and the ceremonies in the Piazza and the Basilica, carried out in the presence of the doge, became an official benediction of a great spiritual enterprise, fraught with danger for those who undertook it. In effect, the Venetian Corpus Christi procession in the Piazza was an imaginative and characteristic exercise in appropriation, made all the more vivid by the presence of the nearby convent of Santo Sepolcro in the Riva degli Schiavoni. This church, which no longer exists, apparently contained a version of the Holy Sepulchre decorated with the inscription 'Hic Intus Est Corpus Iesu Christi' ('Here lies the Body of Jesus Christ'). In addition to being the new Byzantium and the new Rome, Venice had become the new Jerusalem.

6

DECADENCE AND DECLINE

Once did she hold the gorgeous East in fee,
And was the safeguard of the West: the worth
Of Venice did not fall below her birth,
Venice, the eldest child of liberty.
She was a maiden city, bright and free;
No guile seduced, no force could violate;
And when she took unto herself a mate,
She must espouse the everlasting sea.
And what if she had seen those glories fade,
Those titles vanish, and that strength decay,
Yet shall some tribute of regret be paid
When her long life hath reached its final day:
Men are we, and must grieve when even the shade
Of that which once was great has passed away.

William Wordsworth, 'On the Extinction of the Venetian Republic'

In the course of the sixteenth century, English interest in foreign countries, and an awareness of the differences between them, increased enormously. By the time that the scholar William Thomas (d. 1554) published his *Historie of Italy* in 1549, some knowledge of Italy and its customs was already beginning to affect English culture. As the physical appearance of Venice became ever more impressive, so too did its image in the eyes of those who visited it or read about it in guides. Among northerners, curiosity about the Venetian governmental system was keen, fuelled by admiration for its almost mystical independent condition. Suspicion of the more idolatrous aspects of its age-old Catholicism was widespread among Protestants, but this was tempered by a genuine admiration for Venetian wealth and the city's reputation as the home of liberty. In artistic terms the second half of the sixteenth century has often been characterised as a Venetian golden age, with Veronese, Tintoretto and Titian all painting, and architect Andrea Palladio at work. In the Piazza there was the continuing project to complete Sansovino's scheme (Coryate noted that 'the first part of St Markes street is but little more than halfe ended. For it was but lately begun'), but there were also other major projects in progress elsewhere in the city. On the island of San Giorgio Maggiore in the lagoon, directly opposite the Piazzetta, the church begun to Palladio's design in 1565 was finally finished in 1610 with the addition of a façade modelled on the portico of a classical temple, while on neighbouring La Giudecca his church of the Redentore, commissioned in 1577 in thanksgiving for the cessation of a particularly virulent outbreak of plague, was finally completed fifteen years later. Two serious fires which broke out in the Ducal Palace in 1574 and 1577 had been followed by monumental schemes of redecoration of the principal rooms, which elaborate a rich and complex iconography (the results give an intriguing picture of Venetian self-fashioning at the end of the century), and involved some of the most distinguished artists of the day. In the same years, the interior of the Basilica resounded to the sound of the music of Andrea and Giovanni Gabrieli (*c.* 1532–85 and *c.* 1554–1612) and Claudio Monteverdi (1567–1643). These, and other aspects of the cultural life of the times, have given rise to the ubiquitous 'Splendours of Venice' theme so beloved of exhibition curators.

Ironically, given such a rich panorama of artistic activity, the origins of Venetian decline can be traced to precisely the same period. The process has been attributed to a number of factors. As a military and naval force to be reckoned with, Venetian power was now on the wane, and occasional signs to the contrary were seized upon with enthusiasm. The most significant of these – at least in popular mythology – was the victory over the Turks at Lepanto, when, on 7 October 1571, the galleys of Spain, Genoa, Venice and the Papacy, which in the previous year had been formed into a Holy League in response to the Ottoman conquest of Cyprus, fought and defeated the Turkish fleet in the gulf of Corinth. Estimates vary, but about 10,000 Christians died at Lepanto, and perhaps as many as 25,000 Turks, while on the positive side large numbers of Christian slaves who had been put to work in the Turkish galleys were freed. The Spanish writer Miguel de Cervantes (1547–1616), who was wounded during the battle but survived, drew on his experiences in the story 'A Captive's Tale' (1605), just one example from the rich harvest of cultural consequences of the victory which helped to cement Lepanto into place within the evolving Myth of Venice. Notwithstanding contemporary perceptions of its significance, writers since Voltaire have argued that the victory at Lepanto led nowhere. More recently some historians have suggested that a decline in Venetian sea power, accentuated by the increasing strength of the English and the Dutch, was accompanied by an economic recession that reached its height in the early decades of the seventeenth century, while others have noted a turning away from the traditional commercial activities and trade with the East on the part of the patrician classes. In their place the Venetian aristocracy retreated into more locally based activities such as farming and investment in land on the *terraferma*.

Paradoxical though it may seem, little of this was detected by contemporary observers, whether Venetian or foreign. Neither Thomas Coryate, nor the diarist John Evelyn (1620–1706), who arrived in the city in 1645, seems to have found much amiss; for both of them Venice was as resplendent as ever, its physical beauty consolidated by new buildings, its musical life vibrant. In 1608 Coryate set out on the first of his remarkable foreign adventures with the intention to travel continuously for seven years like Ulysses and reach Venice as his final destination. His journey cut short, in 1611 he published an account of his trip, which had been largely carried out on foot. The title of the book, *Coryat's crudities. Hastily gobbled up in five moneths travell etc.*, with an introductory 'Epistle to the Reader' proudly signed 'The Odcombian Legge-Stretcher' (he was born in Odcombe in Somerset), gives a whiff of his curious, exuberant rhetorical style. During another great travelling adventure to Surat, in India, Coryate expired, reputedly from drinking sack while in an enfeebled condition.

Venice itself is the subject of the final chapter of the *Crudities*, where it is ornately presented in rolling prose as the 'fairest Lady, yea the richest Paragon and Queene of Christendome'. Fortunately for us, Coryate explored both the insides and outsides of the buildings that he visited, and was also a witness to a number of special occasions. On one of these, the feast day of Saint Roch on 16 August, he was present in the meeting hall of the Scuola di San Rocco, one of the grandest and wealthiest of the six major confraternities of the city. There, surrounded by Tintoretto's vast glowing canvases which fill up the walls and ceiling, he listened for some three hours to what seems to have been some sort of sacred concert which 'consisted principally of musicke, which was both vocall and instrumental, so good, so delectable, so rare, so admirable, so superexcellent, that it did even ravish and stupifie all those strangers that never heard the like … For mine own part I can say this, that I was for the time even rapt up with Saint Paul into the third heaven.' Coryate's evident enjoyment of music, which comes through so strongly in this passage, also appears in his description of his experiences in San Marco.

Despite their very different characters, both Coryate and Evelyn describe a city densely animated and alive, no more so than in the Piazza San Marco itself. Coryate reserved his most enthusiastic praise for the square, the 'market place of the world', as he called it. On one occasion he encountered the *andata* with, at the centre of the procession, the doge dressed in a rich robe of cloth of silver decorated with 'curious work made in colours with needle-worke'. Venturing into the official buildings ranged around the square, Coryate's sense of wonderment continued to grow. In the Mint he saw its thirty-one chests, filled with gold, silver and brass coins. Entering the Ducal Palace, he wandered around the galleries and staircases in amazement, before happening upon the Hall of the Great Council, 'the fairest that ever I saw in my life, either in mine owne countrey, or France, or any city of Italy, or afterward in Germany. Neither do I thinke that any roome of all Christendome doth excel it in beauty.' Among the many paintings commissioned and installed in the years after the fire of 1577, Coryate singled out for special mention Andrea Vicentino's monumental 1603 canvas of the battle of Lepanto, 'where the Christian fleete got that most glorious victory of the Turkes'. Understandably enough, it was recent events that attracted his attention, rather than distant episodes from Venetian history which he quickly passed over as 'historicall descriptions of many ancient matters'. On the opposite side of the Piazza he entered the library, marvelled at Cardinal Bessarion's collection of books and manuscripts and, in the Antisala, saw 'the little world of memorable antiquities made of Alabaster, and some few in stone, which were brought thither by Cardinall Grimannus, Patriarch of Aquileia'. These were clearly of considerable interest, and in a rather self-satisfied display of classical learning he lists them all.

Standing in front of the façade of the Basilica, Coryate admired the 'four goodly brazen horses made of Corthinian metall, and fully as great as the life', which, he had heard, the Venetians had refused to sell to the king of Spain despite being offered their weight in gold. He also recounts the story of their being made by Lysippus, the legend of their descent from the Emperor Nero to Constantine the Great, and their arrival in Venice from Constantinople. Inside San Marco he heard the 'best musicke that ever I did in all my life', but failed to gain entrance to the Treasury, which was 'very seldome shewed to strangers, but only upon St Markes day'. This was a matter of considerable disappointment since he had heard that 'no treasure whatsoever in any one place of Christendome may compare with it … Here they say is kept marvellous abundance of rich stones of exceeding worth, as Diamonds, Carbuncles, Emerauds, Chrysolites, Jacinths, and great pearles.' In effect this rollcall leaves out much of what is now prized most among the treasures of San Marco, reducing many of the most striking and rare ritual objects to mere baubles, prized for their glitter and monetary value. This is entirely typical of the age. Elizabethan and Jacobean interest in things foreign was often characterised by vulgarity. Works of art were often admired for their materials, and rapturous exclamations over gilding and precious marbles were common.

The same charge could not be directed at John Evelyn, respected in his lifetime as the author of a work on architecture and the translator of another on painting. In his opinion, architecture only became interesting in the late fifteenth century, when it was liberated from gothic models thanks to the influence of classical buildings. In 1643 he set out on a lengthy journey through France and Italy which took him as far south as Naples. Here he enjoyed the best and most plentiful food that he had encountered anywhere on his travels, visited the ruins at Cuma and then returned northwards via Rome, Florence, Bologna, Ferrara and finally Venice. In common with Coryate, Evelyn's most lyrical descriptions are reserved for the Piazza and the Basilica, but unlike Coryate he was able to gain admission to the jealously guarded Treasury with its dazzling array of relics, where he was

> *shewed by a Priest (who first vested himself in his sacerdotals, with the Stola about his neck) the Evangelium of St Mark the Venetian Patron or Tutelarie, affirmed to be written by his owne hand, & whose Body (transported many yeares since*

from Alexandria) they shew buried in this Church: Also a small
Ampulla or glasse of our B. Saviou[r]s blood, as they fancy: A
greate morcell of the real Crosse, one of the nailes, a Thorne, a
fragment of the Column to which our Lord was bound, when
Scourged: The Labbarum or Ensigne (Standard) of victorious
Constantine, a piece of St Lukes arme, a rib of St Stephen, a
finger of Mary Magdalene & a world of Reliquies I could not
remember.

Eighteenth-century Venice is conventionally regarded as
the home of degeneracy. The city's population had declined
from 170,000 at the height of its power to just 96,000 in
1797. Effete aristocrats continued to run the government,
but trade had evaporated, the empire had disintegrated and
the survival of the Republic was largely dependent upon
the good will of neighbouring states. Ostensibly, at least,
foreign visitors, particularly the English, came to Venice for
educational and improving reasons, as part of the Grand
Tour, much as Coryate and Evelyn had done. One of the
ironies attached to the Tour – an extensive experience for the
upper classes normally lasting two or so years – that decisively shaped eighteenth-century British politics and culture
was that the most important guidebook was written by an
expatriate priest, Richard Lassels (*c.* 1603–68), who for most
of his life lived in Rome. And although Rome itself was
the principal destination for this élite, male rite of passage,
through which the young patrician was guided by a knowl-
edgeable tutor, Venice also had its place. In part this was due
to the enduring appeal of the Venetian commonwealth as a
political system; from the late seventeenth century until the
end of the Republic, the image of 'the serene Venetian state'

continued to inspire generations of young milords, both literally and ideologically.

At the same time, it could also lead them astray. Venetian liberty, much admired in the political sphere, often provoked distaste when observed in social behaviour. The reaction of one eighteenth-century English visitor is typical:

> *They [the Venetians] enjoy a sort of liberty but it is only to be libertines and they are grown so scandalous that I think their whole City may well be term'd the Brothell house of Europe, and I dare say virtue was never so out of countenance or vice so encouraged in any part of the World and I believe not in any age as at this time in Venice.*

For many, the seductive lure of Venice in the last decades of the Republic, with her commerce usurped by carnival and her once noble palaces turned into whorehouses, was also subversive. The Piazza was notorious. Fancy goods were sold from little trays by vivacious girls who gathered under the arcades and shimmied between the tables of the coffee houses 'to engage in ribald conversations and behave no better than common courtesans'. There were plenty of those, too, and their touting for business was said to be so invasive that no prosperous-looking man could take half a dozen steps in the square without being approached. The more ingenious women even mixed shopkeeping with streetwalking, to maximise their profits. One secret agent reported in 1766 on

> *a woman called La Sansona with a shop under the Procuratie Vecchie ... quite young, not bad-looking ... most people think her comings and goings with balm and other merchandise are*

cover for something less respectable. A year or two back, every-body knows, she was obviously in want … and now she eats and dresses well. This is all since getting acquainted with many noble patricians …

During the carnival season, which lasted six months, the Piazza became the true centre of activity, dark with pleasure-seekers (one visitor believed there to be as many as 100,000). Cafés and eating houses were open all night, and trinkets were on sale while the mountebanks entertained and the crowds applauded. None the less, time was running out. Those who took their pleasures in Venice, whether citizens or foreigners, English aristocrats or local patricians, did so against the backdrop of a city that, while still energetic, was tangibly decaying. Napoleon was to change all that.

On 17 May 1797, General Baraquay d'Hilliers entered the city with some 7,000 French troops. The Venetians offered no resistance, in fact some positively welcomed the occupiers. Just over a fortnight later the Tree of Liberty, that most potent symbol of the democratic revolution in France, was erected in the Piazza San Marco, now desanctified and to be known as the Piazza Grande. What had once served as the arena for impressive ducal rituals and solemn religious processions became a theatre for patriotic sentiment and political action. At the foot of the Tree agricultural implements, symbols of the prosperity to come under the new régime, were displayed while, to provide the necessary nourishment, members of the Municipality (the new government of the city) threw earth

20. Throughout Napoleon's Italian territories, French officials introduced
the celebratory paraphernalia of the Revolution to signal the beginning of
the new régime. This anonymous engraving shows the Piazza ornamented
with temporary viewing stands with, at its centre, the Tree of Liberty, in
preparation for a celebratory festival.

and water on its roots. Speeches were made and, following the traditional singing of the '*Te Deum*' in the Basilica, a young Venetian couple made their marriage vows. Beginning with a copy of the *Libro d'oro*, and culminating with the ducal insignia (including the doge's golden robes and ermine cape), a collection of objects symbolic of aristocratic power were consigned to the flames of a celebratory pyre and the ashes thrown to the wind. The celebrations ended with dancing. It is said that the Countess Querini-Benzoni, a renowned beauty painted by Pietro Longhi, admired by Stendhal and later to become one of Lord Byron's many Venetian favourites, the 'blonde in the gondola' as the title of a popular song described her, could be seen cavorting around the Tree of Liberty dressed only in a scandalously abbreviated Athenian tunic.

If for liberal Venetians the arrival of Napoleon's men signalled the hope of democratic government, for many there were disadvantages. Nostalgia for the past glories of the Republic was strong, and when the French, following the centuries-old prerogative of victors, began systematically looting the Venetian artistic patrimony, there was a good deal of local unease. As a first step, the French minister Giovanni Battista Lallemont ordered the sequestration of twenty paintings; the task of supervising their shipment to France was placed in the hands of Pietro Edwards, a prominent picture dealer. To these were added others from elsewhere in Italy, including the predella panels from Andrea Mantegna's 1457 San Zeno altarpiece in Verona and antiquities from the Capitoline in Rome. All were taken off to Paris, where they were placed on public display before being hung in the Louvre, soon to be renamed as the Museé Napoleon.

More damaging and controversial in the eyes of many

Venetians was the removal of the four bronze horses from the façade of the Basilica. A number of contemporary engravings and lithographs show them being precariously winched down to the Piazza in front of a large crowd of onlookers, some of the more boisterous of whom are being kept in order by armed militiamen. On their arrival in Paris, official rhetoric justified their transfer as an example of historical inevitability; they were put on show with the explanatory (if inaccurate) caption: 'Brought from Corinth to Rome, and from Rome to Constantinople, from Constantinople to Venice, from Venice to France; they are at last in a Free Country!' Subsequently they were installed on top of the Arc de Triomphe du Caroussel, built between 1806 and 1808 as a grand entrance to the Tuileries palace. The arch itself, based on that of Septimius Severus in Rome, was designed by Charles Percier and Pierre Leonard Fontaine, whose original intention was that a vigorous semi-crouching statue of Napoleon be placed in a chariot driving the horses forward towards the Louvre. One can only assume that this proposal was dropped because of its patent absurdity; even so, the empty chariot still provoked a flurry of puns about *'le char l'attend'* and *'le charlatan'*. In the end, the Arc de Triomphe was officially designated as a celebration of Napoleon's victories of 1805, the events at Trafalgar being conveniently forgotten in the process. Following the return of the horses to Venice, they were replaced by a quadriga, depicting Peace riding in a triumphal chariot guided by winged Victories. In an adroit change of message, the composition transformed the arch from a triumphalist celebration of the military successes of the emperor into a celebration of the restoration of the Bourbons.

Next to be targeted was the Winged Lion of Saint Mark

21. Shortly after their arrival, the French removed the four horses from the façade of the Basilica and transported them to Paris. Some years later they were installed on top of the Arc de Triomphe in the Tuileries facing the Louvre.

22. The Arc de Triomphe du Caroussel was built to commemorate Napoleon's military victories. Following his defeat, and the return of the four horses to Venice, a sculptural ensemble representing Peace riding in a triumphal chariot accompanied by gilded Victories was substituted. The composition, which includes a replacement quadriga inspired by the horses of San Marco, celebrates the restoration of the Bourbons.

(Saint Theodore, whose significance as the earlier patron saint of the city had long been forgotten, remained untouched). This too was taken off to Paris and raised on a pillar in front of the Hôpital des Invalides, 'its tail lowered and placed between its legs as an affront to Venetian grandeur', according to the historian Emmanuele Cicognara. Ideological diehards in the Municipality proposed that the sculptor Antonio Canova (1757–1822), the most acclaimed Italian exponent of the neoclassical style, be commissioned to fashion a statue of Liberty as a substitute, but this came to nothing and, after the demise of the régime, sentiment for this emblem of the past was so strong that a replacement, made of wood covered in copper, was made by a local craftsman and placed on top of the empty column in the Piazzetta. All this and much more (including Veronese's vast canvas painted for the refectory of San Giorgio Maggiore, where it has recently been replaced with a digitally enhanced copy) was taken off to the French capital as cultural booty, some of it never to return, despite agreements about cultural patrimony arrived at by the Congress of Vienna in 1815.

On Lallemont's orders, 500 manuscripts, including an important group of ancient Greek codices from Cardinal Bessarion's donation to the Libreria Sansoviniana, were crated up and despatched to the Bibliothèque Nationale. Items from the Treasury in the Basilica were removed to the Mint, where some were taken to pieces and others melted down; some of the diamonds ended up in Paris, where they were set in Empress Josephine's crown. The kneeling figure of Francesco Foscari was hacked away from its place on the Porta della Carta, not to be replaced until 1885, and the statue of Andrea Gritti on the western façade of the Ducal Palace was smashed.

The *bucintoro*, the elaborately painted and gilded state barge which had been used by the doge on ceremonial occasions – notably the feast of the Ascension, when the Republic was ritually remarried to the Adriatic – was left to rot in its berth in the abandoned Arsenal. This potent symbol of the Republic's maritime greatness now served as an equally powerful image of its decay. As Byron put it in *Childe Harold's Pilgrimage*:

> *The spouseless Adriatic mourns her Lord;*
> *And, annual marriage now no more renewed,*
> *The Bucentaur lies rotting unrestored,*
> *Neglected garment of her widowhood …*

Eventually she was towed out to the lagoon and set on fire in full view of crowds gathered in the Piazzetta and along the Riva degli Schiavoni, though not before the gilding, applied some seventy years before at the staggering cost of 60,000 gold zecchini, had been stripped away. The authorities had considered taking her too to Paris, via Rouen and then down the Seine, but in the end she was judged unfit to travel.

It was shortly after Napoleon's visit in 1807 that a grand scheme for the urban renewal of Venice was drawn up. Some of its guiding principles – the importance of symmetry and the need for public green spaces, in particular – were familiar from the Emperor's plans for Paris. Napoleon had issued ordinances to provide wide thoroughfares culminating in spacious squares and to frame them with ordered, elegant neoclassical façades. In short, the objective was to impose modern theories of urban design, already tried and tested in Paris half a century before Hausmann, on a city whose topographical features were both dictated by and in opposition to nature;

Venice needed to be regulated and controlled, widened and straightened. Some of the more dramatic features of the first Regulatory Plan and its many progeny, such as the ambitious project to create a new piazza twice the size of San Marco on the Giudecca, directly opposite the island of San Giorgio Maggiore, for military parades and other official purposes, eventually came to nothing. Others, notably the scheme to pave over the Rio di Castello, in one of the poorest areas of the city, in order to provide a broad street known as the Via Eugenia in deference to Josephine's son Eugène de Beauharnais (it is now Via Garibaldi) can still be seen. So too can the public gardens, a characteristic Napoleonic touch, which were laid out along its eastern edge, complete with cafés, a trattoria and other pavilions. All this was the work of Giovanni Antonio Selva (1751–1819), the architect of the Fenice theatre, whose original design included an English garden with a raised mound topped by a small temple sheltering a statue of Napoleon, and a public bathhouse.

Given the urban priorities underpinned by political concerns of the French administration, it is not surprising that the focal point of renewal was the Piazza San Marco. Stripped of the more prominent symbols of the old régime, the empty government offices fringing the Piazza and the Piazzetta no longer projected the traditional values of aristocratic authority. In keeping with the imperial rhetoric that had come to typify the metaphors of Napoleonic rule since his coronation in Notre Dame in 1804, it was now decided to transform the Piazza into the site of a royal palace. This was to occupy the whole of the Procuratie Nuove as far as the library on the southern side of the square, and was to extend on the western edge as far as the Procuratie Vecchie. Crucial to the scheme was the demolition of the church of San Geminiano, so that a grand staircase leading to a new ballroom on the first floor could be constructed. The ballroom itself commanded a stunning panorama of the whole square, filled with the bustle of visitors and Venetians alike, taking the *listòn* (the Venetian version of the *passeggiata*), or crowded around the tables in Quadri and Florian. It is claimed, somewhat inconclusively, that it was Napoleon himself who coined the much-repeated description of the Piazza as 'the finest drawing-room in Europe', a phrase echoed by Henry James in *The Aspern Papers* (1888): 'The whole place ... is an open-air salon dedicated to cooling drinks.' This provides both a fitting epitaph and a suitable entrée to Venice's modern existence.

What is sometimes forgotten is that the most recent building in the Piazza is not the Ala Napoleonica, but the Campanile. In the summer of 1902, a menacing crack which had appeared on the north wall of Bartolomeo Bon's much-restored tower continued to expand until, on 14 July, the entire structure collapsed crushing Sansovino's Loggetta in the process. Except for the caretaker's cat no one was killed and, aside from the Loggetta, damage to the surrounding buildings was remarkably limited. Famously, the moment was broadcast around the world in a photograph which later turned out to have been faked; less dramatically, the mountain of rubble which was all that remained was genuinely caught on film. In an emergency meeting held on the same evening the local authorities decided that the Campanile be rebuilt *'com'era, dov'era'* ('as it was, where it was') – the same formula was used by the mayor of Venice, Massimo Cacciari, on the night that the Fenice theatre was burnt to the ground in 1996 – and on the feast of Saint Mark in 1912, exactly 1,000 years after the

23. On 14 July 1902 the Campanile collapsed, damaging the northern corner of Sansovino's library and crushing the Loggetta. At a meeting held the same evening, the City Council resolved that a copy should be built in its place, faithful in its external details to the original, while using lighter materials and modern techniques of construction. The bells, all but one of which were shattered, were recast from the original metal and presented to Venice by Pope Pius X.

foundations of the original structure had been allegedly laid, the new tower was inaugurated in a ceremony which was turned into a major state occasion. Shock and disbelief had accompanied the collapse. The durability of Venetian buildings, a symbol of the Republic itself, had become legendary. 'Even the humblest seem constructed for eternity, not time,' wrote the American consul in 1853, and the phrase *'incrollabile come il Campanile di San Marco'* ('indestructible as the bell tower of San Marco') was a popular Venetian saying. The reconstruction of the original tower, which had to be done from old photographs since neither plans nor drawings existed, was portrayed as the expression of a preserved and revived Venice within a resurgent Italy. In turn, this replica has generated further offspring, particularly in North America. The clock tower of King Street Station in Seattle, the MetLife Tower in New York City and Sather Tower on the campus of the University of California in Berkeley are all inspired to some extent by the original in the Piazza San Marco, Venice. Even more so is the building designed for the Kroch banking house in Leipzig, constructed in 1928. Originally the scheme also included flagpoles in front of the nearby opera house, while the bells on top of the tower clearly resonate with their Venetian prototype, and the lions on the façade conveniently occur in the city's coat of arms. The benign inscription of the Torre dell'Orologio (*'Horas non numero nisi serenas'*, 'Recording only the happy hours', has been converted to the more severe and unsmiling injunction *'Labor Vincit Omnia'* ('Labour Conquers All Things'). In the following decades, as Venice reinvented itself yet again in the wake of its complete loss of any political authority, questions of fakes, facsimiles and fantasy were to recur with some regularity.

24. Hans Kroch, a Leipzig banker, was responsible for the construction of an eleven-storey steel-reinforced tower in the centre of the city in 1928. The east face of the building is decorated with a clock, while two figures on the roof strike the bells every quarter of an hour. The design, which also incorporates two reliefs of lions (the symbol of Leipzig as well as Venice), is clearly indebted to the Torre dell' Orologio in the Piazza.

....

FROM SPRITZ TO PINK FLOYD

Water and marble and that silentness
Which is not broken by a wheel or hoof;
A city like a water-lily, less
Seen than reflected, palace wall and roof,
In the unfruitful waters motionless,
Without one living grass's green reproof;
A city without joy or weariness,
Itself beholding, from itself aloof.

Arthur Stevens, 'Venice'

In June 1814, following a short siege, the city of Venice fell to the Austrians, and Venetia and Lombardy were duly annexed to the Hapsburg Empire. At first the signs were encouraging. No sensible Venetian believed that the Republic could be restored to its former glory (in reality the halcyon days of the fifteenth and sixteenth centuries, rather than the *status quo* in 1797), and almost anything seemed preferable to life under the Napoleonic boot. Most citizens were preoccupied with the conditions of everyday existence, but there were also other considerations. One of the initiatives taken at the Congress of Vienna was that works of art stolen from Italy during the Napoleonic period be repatriated. This enlightened resolution, which effectively introduced a new concept of patrimony (if only between the European powers), was the culmination of a long campaign for their restitution which, after some prevarication on the part of the French, was only made possible through the intervention of Prince Klemens Wenzel von Metternich with the assistance of Austrian troops. Forcibly removed from their home on the Arc du Caroussel in 1815, and then crated up with paintings from the nearby Louvre, the four bronze horses finally reached Venice in the same year. Following hurried restoration, they were ceremonially raised back to their original position on the façade of the Basilica on 13 December, eighteen years to the day after they had been removed. The Emperor Francis I (1768–1835), who was in attendance, decreed that an inscribed tablet be placed over the west door recording the Austrian role in their repatriation.

In the following year the Lion of Saint Mark, which had been inadvertently smashed into eighty-four separate fragments during its transfer from Paris and had undergone extensive restoration in the foundries of the Arsenal as a result, was reinstated on top of its column in the Piazzetta. Taken together, these two highly visible public acts benefited the new administration in a number of ways. Firstly, they demonstrated that Austrian resolve over the question of artistic heritage, so much in evidence at the Congress, could be put into practice. In addition, in a politically adroit move, the Austrians impressed upon the Venetians both their sense of respect for the past and their determination to reverse some of the more damaging consequences of the French occupation. Similar motivations are evident in some of the other projects put in hand elsewhere in the vicinity of the Piazza.

In the new reception rooms of the Palazzo Reale, whose ceilings had already been partly frescoed under the French, the decorations were continued, eradicating in the process all references to Napoleon and replacing them with traditional mythological iconography. To the rear of the building work continued Napoleon's project to transform the spaces cleared by the demolition of the old gothic granaries of the Republic, visible in Jacopo de' Barbari's map, into a new garden, the Giardinetti Reali. Lorenzo Santi (1783–1839), the architect placed in charge of these schemes, having originally been appointed by the French, failed with his proposal to dignify the old Ponte della Pescaria with a colonnade and statues, but succeeded in his plans for a small pavilion in the southwestern corner of the garden. Designed as a caffè, and based on the traditional design of a triumphal arch, it is crowned by a small drum and shallow dome. A garden casino of conventional type, it is the most exquisite example of the neoclassical manner to be found anywhere in Venice.

Despite these architectural indicators of rejuvenation, Venice was dying, both literally and metaphorically. The few trappings of the period of the doges that had not been suppressed, destroyed, sold off or looted were now disposed of or left to rot. Paintings and furniture were auctioned off by the old aristocracy, to be snapped up by English and French collectors, as many families disposed of their palaces and left. The Venetian fleet, which Napoleon had actually tried to strengthen, was sold off to Denmark since the Hapsburgs had no need of it, a decision which finally marked the end of a thousand-year presence in the Mediterranean. Just ten years after the Austrians arrived in 1813, the population had shrunk to 113,827, 10 per cent down from the 137,240 souls

25. Lorenzo Santi's coffeehouse stands next to the gardens (the Giardinetti Reali) which lie beyond the Mint and alongside the lagoon. These were laid out during the Napoleonic occupation of Venice in order to free up the view of the water from the Procuratie Nuove.

registered when the French took over seven years before. In the Arsenal, once the largest industrial complex in Europe, the workforce dwindled from 3,302 to a mere 773 over the same period. More shockingly, more than one third of Venetians were officially recognised as being 'in receipt of public assistance'. The poet Percy Bysshe Shelley, in 'Written among the Euganean Hills', sensed the atmosphere of nostalgia and decline in lines which resonate with the centuries-old image of Venice, queen of the Adriatic:

Sun-girt city, thou hast been
Ocean's child, and then his queen;
Now is come a darker day,
And thou soon must be his prey.

In this city of diminished importance, denuded of political significance, economic vitality and even the last visible vestiges of the naval strength on which its economic superiority had once been based, the benevolent toleration which at first had greeted newcomers gradually gave way to mutual suspicion and hostility, as the bureaucratic structures of occupation were slowly put into place. In England, the editor of the *Quarterly Review* wrote that 'life had gradually ebbed from the extremities and seemed to flutter but faintly in its last retreat at the heart of the city, the Piazza of St Mark's'. As the authorities set about a rigid and systematic policy of germanisation, there turned out to be little sympathy for existing traditions and practices. Spies were everywhere and censorship oppressive. At the Fenice theatre, the principal venue for opera in the city, and traditionally a social magnet for the smart set, the Austrian censor was busy at work with the blue pencil of intolerance. When, in 1833, Gioachino Rossini's *William Tell* (1829) was performed there, the designation of the role of Gessler, portrayed in the work as a ruthless autocrat, was altered from 'governor' to the more anodyne 'administrator'. Three years later, performances of the work were banned completely in case its glorification of Swiss independence should encourage the Venetians to harbour rebellious ideas.

Informers lurked under the arcades in the Piazza, and conversations between groups of wealthy Venetians gathered in the cafés in the square were duly overheard and reported, but nothing of moment was discovered; according to official police reports, everything was discussed except politics. More than anything else, it was the severity of the censor and the omnipresence of the secret police that were to give rise to the black legend of Austrian oppression, one of the main structural supports of Risorgimento historiography. In this version of events, the Piazza became a political symbol, the focus of revolt. What is sometimes overlooked in the evolution of this potent piece of mythology, particularly by early historians of a united Italy, is that the Austrians brought the benefits of efficiency and modernisation to Venice as, in the last decades of their administration, a measure of prosperity returned and the economic depression gradually began to recede. Parts of the city were renovated, gaslight was introduced, and repairs to the urban fabric carried out. In 1846, just two years before Daniele Manin's (1804–57) disastrous if spirited revolt against the Hapsburg administration took place, engineers slung a massive stone bridge across the lagoon, greatly reducing, both materially and psychologically, Venetian isolation from both the mainland and the rest of the world. From now on, many visitors would gain their first glimpse of Venice not from a

26. Throughout its history the Piazza was often the stage for political action. Daniele Manin's failed revolt against the Austrian occupation of Venice began here in 1848.

gondola gliding slowly and gently across the lagoon, but from the window of a railway carriage. As the British artist, writer and historian John Ruskin (1819–1900) (not an admirer of the invention) was one of the first to notice, with this bold entry into the steam age, more than a little of the old magic, which he had experienced for the first time when his parents had first brought him to Venice, had disappeared. 'All the romance of it is gone, and nothing that I see ever makes me forget that I am in the nineteenth century,' he wrote to his father. Not entirely truthfully as it transpired, but certainly some of the enchantment had evaporated. Fellow antiquarians and nostalgics apart, as the reality of the city diminished, its magical qualities only increased.

Although Ruskin was to become the most influential of all those who studied and wrote about Venice in the nineteenth century, this age of the city as a magic kingdom, it was Hester Piozzi (1741–1821) (better known as Mrs Thrale), a friend of Dr Johnson, who first introduced English readers to the idea of Venice as the ultimate enchanted city. For her the Piazza was, above all, a magical pleasureground: 'adorned with every excellence of human art and pregnant pleasure, expressed by intelligent countenances sparkling with every grace of nature, the sea washing its walls, the moonbeams dancing on its subjugated waves, sport and laughter resounding from the coffeehouses, girls with guitars skipping about the square, masks and merry-makers singing as they pass you'. In common with many earlier English visitors who had been intrigued by the Venetian political system and by the architecture of the city as an expression of the virtues of republican rectitude, she admiringly claimed that the Venetians had 'preserved their laws inviolate, their city unattempted, and their republic respectable, through all the concussions that have shaken the rest of Europe' (distant echoes here of Petrarch). But Mrs Thrale's most lyrical praise was reserved for a poetic vision of a Venice undisturbed by the imminence of its destruction. On a clear night she experienced 'the general effect produced by such architecture, such painting, such pillars, illuminated as I saw them last night by the moon at full, rising out of the sea', which 'produced an effect like enchantment'. Following the departure of the French in 1814 and the Austrians in 1866, Venice entered upon a new existence as a strange and fantastical spectacle, curiously marooned from reality.

As such the city became a central locus for the European imagination. The idea of Venice as the site of such emotions is one of the major themes of nineteenth-century descriptions of the city. From Mrs Thrale its descent can be traced to Byron, and from there to the painter J. M. W. Turner and Ruskin and then on to the French writer Marcel Proust. If for Byron Venice was simply the most beautiful ruin that ever existed, for Turner it was a city dissolving into light. As for Ruskin, on his first visit in 1841 he became enraptured with Venice and its architecture to the extent that, forty years later, when the effort of writing *Praeterita* (1885–9) had brought him to the point of mental collapse, he feverishly recalled the excitement of that first encounter. Writing to his Venetian friend Count Alvise Zorzi, Ruskin placed the Piazza at the heart of his recollections. Using the 'Pillars of Acre' themselves as a kind of descriptive fulcrum, he imaginatively recreated in his mind's eye the Basilica with its shimmering interior, the Ducal Palace with the lagoon beyond, and the square itself:

Of all the happy and ardent days which, in my earlier life, it was granted to me to spend in this Holy Land of Italy, none were so precious as those which I used to spend in the bright recess of your Piazzetta, by the pillars of Acre; looking sometimes to the glimmering mosaics in the vaults of the Church; sometimes to the Square, thinking of its immortal memories; sometimes to the Palace and the Sea. No such scene existed elsewhere in Europe, – in the world; so bright, so magically visionary, – a temple radiant as the flowers of nature, venerable and enduring as her rocks, arched above the rugged pillars which stood simply on the marble pavement, where the triumphant Venetian conqueror had set them.

A few years later Ruskin returned to Venice with his 20-year-old wife Effie, and put up at the Hotel Danieli on the Riva degli Schiavoni. From their window they could see the Campanile, from which it was only a short walk to the Piazza itself. Damage caused by the Austrian siege which had brought Manin's short-lived republic to such an abrupt end was everywhere to be seen. So, too, were the Austrian troops now garrisoned in Venice, and from under the arcades of the Ducal Palace artillery was kept permanently trained on the Piazzetta as the most likely landing stage for Italian patriot Giuseppe Garibaldi's freedom fighters. On arrival the Ruskins had discovered that the new railway connecting Venice to the mainland had been destroyed and, fearful for the fate of the most important buildings in the city, Ruskin set out on a systematic tour of inspection. While Effie moved effortlessly in the higher reaches of society, in particular among the officers of the occupying forces (in a fiercely divided Venice the Ruskins were on the side of the Austrians), John preferred to pursue his researches into Venetian architecture, attracting a mixture of curiosity and bewilderment as he went about drawing, measuring and struggling through the crowded alleyways and squares with cumbersome photographic equipment, diligently sizing up cusps and corbels. As the scholar and critic Tony Tanner eloquently put it in *Venice Desired*, 'his business was with those under-canal vaults and mud-buried porticos ... for Ruskin seems to have literally crawled and climbed over the whole ruined body of a city; peering with his incomparable eye into every darkened and neglected nook and cranny, high and low; gently picking over the abandoned stones of decaying palaces; gliding into and down the darkest and dingiest canals'. Ruskin was to return on a number of occasions, until his technical and critical approach to Venetian architecture culminated in an almost military campaign of methodical intense study in the winter of 1849. As he put it, 'it became necessary for me to examine not only every one of the older palaces, stone by stone, but every fragment throughout the city which afforded any clue to the formation of its styles'. The phrase 'stone by stone' is revealing. Beyond the accuracy and beauty of Ruskin's drawings and watercolours of Venetian buildings, there is a quite intense and novel attention to the material character of the stones themselves, not only to the way in which they had been cut, but also to qualities of texture and colour as they were revealed in different lights. Hence the title of the most inspiring guidebook to Venice ever to have been written, *The Stones of Venice* (1851–3).

Tension was in the air, particularly in the Piazza, and Ruskin noticed it. The Austrian military band that, strategically placed in the very centre of the Piazza, played daily, competing with the music from the Basilica and drowning out the sound of choir and organ during the liturgical services, was an aural symbol of subjugation, dominating the soundscape and obliterating tradition. Italian patriots and sympathisers left as soon as it started to play. Ruskin caught both the social detail and the brooding atmosphere:

> *Round the whole square in front of the church there is almost a continuous line of cafés, where the idle Venetians of the middle classes lounge, and read empty journals: in the centre the Austrian bands play during the time of vespers, their martial music jarring with the organ's notes – the march drowning the* Miserere, *and the sullen crowd thickening round them – a crowd, which, if it had its will, would stiletto every soldier that pipes to it. And in the recesses of the porches, all day long, knots of men of the lowest classes, unemployed and listless, lie basking in the sun like lizards; and unregarded children, every heavy glance of their young eyes full of desperation and stony depravity, and their throats hoarse with cursing – gamble, and fight, and snarl, and sleep, hour after hour, clashing their* centesimi *upon the marble ledges of the church porch.*

The atmosphere of hostility towards the Austrian officers who 'floated about … like oil on water', and the extraordinary rift between the Venetians and the authorities, was also noticed by the German composer Richard Wagner (1813–88) who, sitting at the window of a restaurant in the Piazza, was suddenly startled to hear one of his own overtures:

> *I did not know which dazzled me most, the incomparable Piazza magnificently illuminated and filled with countless numbers of*

moving people, or the music that seemed to be borne away in
rustling glory to the winds. Only one thing was wanting that
might certainly have been expected from an Italian audience: the
people were gathered round listening most intently, but no two
hands ever forgot themselves so far as to applaud, as the least
sign of approbation of Austrian military music would have been
looked upon as treason to the Italian Fatherland.

Wagner, who was rarely 'dazzled' by anything not of his
own doing, also noticed a procession of clerics in their vestments passing along the Piazza San Marco accompanied by a
band of onlookers who could barely conceal their disdain. To a
much greater extent than ever before in its long history, Venice
was now a secular city. This is not to say that the Venetian
taste for impressive spectacles had been entirely lost, despite
the suppression of many traditional festivities (though not
carnival) by the French and the Austrians. One of the grandest occasions of all, rivalling even the entry of Napoleon, took
place just a couple of years after Venice became part of the
Regno d'Italia. On the twentieth anniversary of his failed
uprising against the Austrians, the body of Manin, who had
died in Paris in 1857, was repatriated in a piece of carefully
orchestrated ceremonial worthy of the heyday of the Republic itself. The great patriot's remains were brought along the
Grand Canal from the railway station to the Piazza by night,
accompanied by hundreds of gondolas and small craft. Illuminated by torches, the barge which carried them was decorated with bronze statues representing Venice being consoled
by a newly unified Italy. At the Piazzetta, where an official
guard of honour had been drawn up, the coffin was placed
on a platform at the foot of the Campanile. Then, following

a lying-in-state, during which the Venetians queued in their thousands to pay their respects, a second funeral was conducted in San Marco. Manin's body was finally placed to rest in a sarcophagus situated on the north side of the Basilica, facing the Piazzetta dei Leoncini.

It is difficult to overestimate the significance of this event. The processional life for which the city had been famous for centuries had effectively come to an end with the fall of the Republic. Since then there had been few grand spectacles in the Piazza and, inevitably, all of those were connected to the preoccupations and achievements of the occupying forces. Most impressive of all had been the arrangements made for Napoleon's visit to the city in 1807, a politically contrived occasion which served to consolidate a second period of French rule. Although his visit served to revive the ceremonial of the Republic in all its grandeur, there were a number of important divergences from tradition. In place of the defunct *bucintoro*, Napoleon was rowed down the Grand Canal in a specially commissioned gilded barge. More importantly, on arrival at the Piazzetta, he disembarked not to enter the Ducal Palace, but to go to the Palazzo Reale in the Procuratie Nuove. In doing so, he signalled the importance of the plan of urban renewal that was to be announced shortly after his visit, and which had at its heart the remodelling of the western end of the Piazza.

Perhaps unwittingly, Napoleon also briefly participated in the debate between gothic and classical architectural styles which was heralded by this transformation. John Ruskin's lifelong involvement with Venice was with a city declining to the point of disappearance. In the years after Manin's failed revolution Venice became desolate, its churches emptied and its palaces closed up as the aristocracy moved to the mainland. Carnival collapsed, and even the grander buildings began to show signs of decay and dereliction. The Fenice theatre went dark for eight years in 1858, and opportunities for public celebration were sullenly ignored by both the cognoscenti and wealthy alike. The traditional sounds of the Piazza evaporated, to be replaced by military marches and occasional shouts of protest against the Austrians. In this sombre atmosphere (there was 'no greater social dullness, on land or sea, than in contemporary Venice', the American writer William Howells (1837–1920) warned his readers), Ruskin earnestly began his mission 'to trace the lines of this image before it be forever lost, and to record, as far as I may, the warning which seems to be uttered by every one of the fast-gaining waves, that beat like passing bells, against the STONES OF VENICE'. It is not surprising, given his views of the decadence of the Renaissance, corrupted by rationalism and the weakening of religious belief in the face of scientific enquiry, that for him the Doge's Palace – or, to be more precise, its gothic version begun under Doge Ziani in 1301 – was the most significant building not just in the Piazza, or even in Venice, but in the world. The palace 'stands comparatively alone, and fully expresses the "Gothic power"', since 'the majesty of this single building was able to give pause to the Gothic imagination in its full career; stayed the restlessness of innovation in an instant, and forbade the powers which have created it thenceforth to exert themselves in new directions, or endeavours to summon an image more attractive'. For Ruskin this was perfection achieved in a void, 'the great and sudden invention of one man …[since] there is literally *no* transitional form between [earlier buildings] and the perfection of the Ducal Palace …'

'The Ducal Palace is the Parthenon of Venice and Gradenigo its Pericles.' If, by his own admission, 'it was the determination of this one fact which occupied the greater part of the time I spent in Venice', Ruskin's admiration for the Basilica was at times even more rapturous. In what must be counted as the most lyrical description of the west façade in all literature, Ruskin concentrates on the 'sculpture fantastic and involved, of palm leaves and lilies, and grapes and pomegranates, and birds clinging and fluttering among the branches, all twined together into an endless network of buds and plumes; and in the midst of it, the solemn forms of angels, sceptred, and robed to the feet … And round the walls of the porches there are set pillars of variegated stones, jasper and porphyry, and deep-green serpentine spotted with flakes of snow and marbles, that half refuse and half yield to the sunshine …'

For many, Ruskin's sense of wonder could be translated into the simple commonplace of the tourist guidebooks; Venice had, in Benjamin Disraeli's phrase, 'been raised from the spoils of the teeming Orient'. This perception, affirmed in Wordsworth's celebration of the Republic's imperial dominion over 'the gorgeous East', was used to explain everything about the medieval architecture of the Piazza that was thought to be unusual, strange or exotic. 'I cannot help thinking St Mark's a mosque,' wrote the English travel writer William Beckford (1760–1844), 'and the neighbouring palace some vast seraglio, full of arabesque saloons, embroidered sofas, and voluptuous Circassians.'

The influence of Ruskin's Venice was enormous. Henry James, who wrote about the city in *The Aspern Papers* and *The Wings of the Dove* (1902), arrived there aged 26 with a copy of

Ruskin in his luggage. Proust, who reviewed a translation of *The Stones* in 1906, and who visited Venice for the first time in the spring of the year in which Ruskin died, declared that 'Ruskin made the world beautiful for me'. Somewhat more prosaically, the American poet Ezra Pound some years later declared the city to be 'an excellent place to come from Crawfordsville, Indiana ... more agreeable than Wyncote, Pa., or "47th" and Madison Avenue', and, in a passage strongly evocative of Ruskin's own image of the Basilica, described San Marco as a 'glorious Bible ... in which the skill and the treasures of the East had gilded every letter, and illuminated every page, till the Book-Temple shone from afar off like the star of the Magi ... the precious binding, in the finest Cordoba leather, of the colossal Gospel of Venice'. By now, in the wake of the Austrian withdrawal, Venice had recovered some of its legendary festivity and cultural vitality and, from the 1870s until the Great War, the city became once more a centre of fashion and modernity. Renewed interest in the city produced the international campaign to halt the programme of restoration of the Ducal Palace and the Basilica. This had been going on unnoticed for some forty years, but in that time fashions had changed from admiration for recreation in the spirit of the old in the manner of gothic revivalist Eugène Viollet-le-Duc, to respect for the aesthetics of decay. When the hoardings came down from the southern side of the Basilica to reveal scrubbed columns and freshly cut stone, the artistic élites of the English-speaking world rose to their feet. 'The effect produced,' complained Henry James, 'is that of witnessing a forcible maquillage of one's grandmother ... [it is] a sight to make angels howl.'

Others were less bothered. For Arthur Symons, the

English high priest of Decadence, Venice was a theatre of masks, and the Piazza nothing less than a stage set, the spiritual and physical centre of the city. 'I seemed, after all, not to have left London,' he wrote, 'but to be still at the Alhambra, watching a marvellous ballet ... The Doge's Palace looked exactly like a beautifully painted canvas, as if it were stretched on frames, and ready to be shunted into the wings.' Symons saw a stage that was empty – 'the actors, the dancers, are gone' – but it was not to be deserted for long. Writing on the eve of the First World War, Pound commented on the swank and sophistication of the Piazza, which 'seemed yesterday like one large Carlton Hotel'. Henry James, whose use of domestic imagery reveals a similar view of Venice as a place of modishness and distinction, famously described the square as 'a smooth-floored chamber of amenity', 'an immense open-air drawing room'. Initially, the war itself made little impact on the appearance of the square, though the horses were lowered from the terrace for safekeeping, and the more fragile monuments protected by sandbags. By night the tables under the arcades were still crowded even though the tourists had long gone, but all this was to change as the Austrians intensified their aircraft raids over the city. A marble plaque bearing the stark and terrifying reminder BOMBA AUSTRIACA still marks the spot where an incendiary bomb fell just yards from the main door of the Basilica. Once the war was over, the visitors returned, Venice took up its old habits, and the ordeals of wartime were forgotten. In 1922 the Italian writer Ugo Ojetti watched the shooting of *I due Foscari*, the first of many films to use the square as a backdrop, reliving in the process Symons's experience of the real becoming fake.

The shifting crowds of strangers that have shuffled through

27. The Piazza in time of war. In this photograph, taken in June 1915, the arches of the ground floor Loggia of the Ducal Palace are strengthened with brick piers, while the sculpture of Adam and Eve on the corner facing the Piazzetta is surrounded by wooden scaffolding. These safety measures, designed to protect the building against aerial bombing, remained in place until 1919.

the Piazza in recent times have left cultural traces that have little to do with Venetian history or customs, from the expensive if bogus Viennese ambience of the Caffè Florian, a rococo stage set within a Renaissance theatre, where the classic drink is a 'Spritz' – a mixture of Campari and prosecco, introduced by the Austrians in the nineteenth century – to the faint sounds, drifting in from under the arches of the Procuratie Vecchie, of retired opera singers pumping out the popular Neapolitan song 'O sole mio'. The many and varied uses, not all of them decorous, to which the Piazza has been put over the centuries, from the bull-running contests and ducal processions of the Renaissance, via eighteenth-century carnival jinks to the commercialised nostalgia of today, has helped to establish its status as the ultimate piazza, an accolade that was confirmed on 15 July 1989, when the band Pink Floyd played before an audience of 200,000 gathered there. Appropriately enough, the the star number of the evening was 'Money'.

Piazza San Marco has now entered upon a post-modern existence, where the key elements are tourists, pigeons and reciprocal sociability. Occasionally the enterprise is baptised by the *acqua alta*, the high tides that flood the low-lying areas of the city, including the Piazza, on a regular basis throughout the winter and spring. A long-standing phenomenon, it has grown very considerably in both frequency and depth since the Second World War. Its most dramatic manifestation occurred on 4 November 1966, the same day that the river Arno famously overflowed its banks in Florence, but there have been a number of other bad moments. The most recent took place on 1 December 2008, when the waters rose 1.56 metres above sea level and boys on motorised surfboards skimmed through the square like waterborne ballerinas.

28. The famous Caffè Florian, mentioned by distinguished travellers and writers, stands under the porticos of the Procuratie Nuove. Its eighteenth-century interior, restructured in the following century, consists of a sequence of elegantly decorated rooms.

None of these three features are newcomers to the square, but all have now been conceptualised afresh. Pigeons are perhaps the easiest of these defining characteristics to deal with. Their presence in the Piazza allegedly has a long history. According to one legend they are there because Doge Enrico Dandolo sent back news of the fall of Constantinople by carrier pigeon. According to another, Venetian pigeon worship derives from the Palm Sunday procession in the Piazza during the time of the Republic, when birds were released from the roof of the Basilica, their legs weighted down with paper crowns so that they could be caught by the spectators, killed and finally eaten as a festive delicacy on Easter Sunday. Whatever the explanation, they have survived and prospered, if only thanks to the corn provided until recently by tourists (both the feeding of pigeons and the sale of pigeon food in the Piazza has been forbidden since 2008). As the Baedeker guidebook airily puts it, 'those whose ambitions lean in that direction may have themselves photographed covered with the birds'.

Of the three features, tourism is the most significant, at least visually and economically. Philippe de Commynes, Richard Guylforde, Coryate, Ruskin, Wagner, Turner (the rollcall is impressive and endless), all of these were newcomers to Venice and the Piazza and, fortunately for us, intelligent and careful observers of what they found there. As has so often been said, Venice is rarely written about from the inside, but is appropriated from without. For the post-Napoleon generation of Byron and Shelley, Venice was remote, isolated and largely abandoned, a city ripe for the poetic imagination. All that was to change with the intrusion of the modern world. Even by the time of Ruskin's first visits, Venice had

29. A long-standing problem, with every season that passes the *acqua alta* becomes more frequent and more damaging. Venice is now subject to flooding on more than two hundred days in the year, compared to just seven when this photograph was taken. Work has now started on the Moses Project, which involves seventy-eight steel barriers lying on the sea bed, to be activated during exceptionally high tides.

become a repopulated city, significantly devoted to tourism. In publisher John Murray's *Handbook for Travellers in Northern Italy* of 1842, the visitor is already urged to pay attention to individual monuments, stripped of their historical contexts and sometime political significance. By 1846, the year in which the city was linked to Vicenza by rail, there were eleven hotels of note in Venice, including the Danieli where John and Effie Ruskin spent their disastrous honeymoon. By 1857 the railway had been completed as far as Milan, and Venice had been brought within easy reach of travellers from England and France. By 1848, when an outdoor bathing pool was established at the mouth of the Grand Canal, the local economy was lifting and the tourist trade was clearly beginning to assume a significant role. As one contemporary report put it, the site had been chosen for 'the depth and flow of the water and the magical views of the nearby Piazza San Marco ... the service is run with great care and *politesse*, with the women separated from the men'. With this simple initiative the phenomenon of mass tourism in Venice may be said to have been baptised. The first Cook's tour took place in 1867, and by 1881 Henry James was already lamenting the presence of guides 'lead[ing] their helpless captives through churches and galleries in dense, irresponsible groups'.

Venice has now reached bursting point. Twelve million visitors, it has been estimated, now move through and around the Piazza every year, with the result that the Venetians themselves (those that remain; the population has diminished to 60,000) avoid it if possible. Although tourism in some dimension has been a feature of the square from the beginning of its existence, from the sociological point of view the successors of Ruskin, Byron and James seem to have different concerns and motivations. In 1993 just over 1 million people visited the Ducal Palace, while the Museo Correr in the Piazza, which boasts some of the most exquisite art in Venice, had only 65,000 admissions in the same year. This is where sociability comes in, since it seems that the hordes that now congregate in the square have become something of an attraction in themselves; the main reason to be there is not to explore the buildings, but to have 'done Venice', to participate in the sense of being in the right place as defined by tourist guides ('the piazza par excellence ... without an equal in the world', as the *Blue Guide* puts it). Until recently the atmosphere of the kasbah that the Piazza had become at midday in the spring and summer was squalid, with back-packers encamped between the orchestras playing Strauss waltzes while the pigeons swooped threateningly overhead. Under the porticos of the Ducal Palace and on the steps of the Procuratie Nuove the relics of hastily improvised meals from paper bags – sandwiches, bottles, greasy paper, salami, ham, crisps, ice creams – were everywhere to be seen. In the face of this degradation, the authorities seemed to be as incapable of action as were the sixteenth-century procurators tasked with clearing away drinking dens and food stalls to make way for Sansovino's grand scheme. Recently the situation has improved, if only slightly. In September 2007, the mayor of Venice, Massimo Cacciari, established a squad of volunteers of all ages – housewives, pensioners and students – whose job it is to persuade tourists not to picnic in the Piazza, or to go around bare-chested, or to leave bottles under the arcades, or to throw food containers on to the ground. Those who refuse the invitation to behave decorously risk being fined.

For some, salvation of quite another kind may be at hand.

These days, at least for North Americans, it is no longer necessary to make the long, uncomfortable and disorienting flight to Marco Polo airport (the Venetian sense of a past dominated by intrepid mercantile adventurers never dies) in order to get a whiff of the real thing. According to appreciative reviews posted on its website, the Venetian is 'another luxurious hotel along Las Vegas Boulevard', where 'you can admire wonderful old world European architecture as colourful gondoliers guide tourists along canals of unnaturally [sic] blue water'. Once inside, the visitor is enveloped by an enormous shopping arcade, 'where the a/c will keep you cool but you will still feel like you're outdoors under the ceilings of painted clouds'. On all sides stand copies of prominent Venetian buildings, while at the very heart of this phantasmagorical facsimile, just as in the original, is the Piazza, 'an almost exact scaled replica (170 yards long and 80 yards wide) of the real one in Venice, Italy'. Here you can 'grab a seat' (not possible, after all, in the original) 'and wait for the next free performance of Italian opera singers or living statues.' An even more gargantuan replica, modelled on the Las Vegas example, has now been opened in Macao as 'a renaissance Venice-themed property featuring stunning replicas of Venetian landmarks'. As if in recognition of its own geographical location, and in defiance of the alleged homogenisation of the planet brought about by McDonaldisation, the Macau version of the Venetian is enlivened with a few touches of local colour: 'Chinese-style sampans as well as gondolas sail down canals, bringing the charm of Venice and the glamour of Las Vegas'. Notice that not even the sampans are genuine, adding the final layer to a multiple palimpsest of fakes, rather like a complicated archaeological site where traces of successive cultures have been piled one on top of another.

There is a footnote to this long history, which begins with the delineation of a public arena for political decision and communal ceremony in the early middle ages. In a neat piece of ironic counterpoint, the London *Daily Telegraph* published two stories, side by side, about the use of electricity and its ecological consequences in its morning edition of 14 September 2008. In the first, the paper announced that 'The Eiffel Tower is to lose its sparkle as thousands of its twinkling light bulbs are cut in a new green initiative'. This, apparently, is '*pour encourager les autres*' more than anything; as a spokesman for the mayor of Paris explained, 'it's above all a symbolic decision, as the cost savings are not enormous'. A few hundred miles to the south, considerations of cost are also evidently paramount, but in a different sense. 'City councillors in Venice,' the *Telegraph* reported, 'are planning to cast aside 900 years of history and erect electronic billboards in St Mark's Square.' Since the 1950s, plans have been afoot to restore three of the most imposing buildings in the Piazza – the Biblioteca Nazionale Marciana, the Ala Napoleonica and the Mint. Now that the project is finally to start, it is proposed to position electronic screens in front of the façades to hide the operation. The visual effect, which will undoubtedly be with us for some years, will give this most iconic of spaces an appearance reminiscent of Times Square or Piccadilly Circus. As things stand, the façade of Sansovino's library is already embalmed in a strident advocacy for the latest proposal from the Swiss watch company Swatch: '007 Villain Collection', it proclaims, 'The spy who loved me/Jaws'. (The English language, even if used incomprehensibly, is *de rigueur* in current Italian publicity campaigns for almost anything.) On the other side of the Piazzetta, the eastern corner of the Doge's

30. The library in the Piazzetta, 2009. Breaking with established convention, it has now been agreed that advertising, if only temporary while renovation goes on behind, is to be allowed in the Piazzetta.

Palace is shrouded in a noisy advertisement for an upmarket Italian car manufacturer: 'Lancia Delta – The Power to be Different.'

Ruskin would have been appalled. Perhaps, at least for a few years, it will have to be Las Vegas after all.

APPENDIX I

....

DOGES OF VENICE

697–717	Paoluccio Anafesto
717–26	Marcello Tegalliano
726–37	Orso Ipato
737–42	[Interregnum]
742–55	Teodato Ipato
755–6	Galla Gaulo
756–64	Domenico Monegario
764–87	Maurizio Galbaio
787–804	Giovanni Galbaio
804–11	Obelario degli Antenori
811–27	Agnello Particiaco
827–9	Giustiniano Particiaco
829–36	Giovanni I Particiaco
836–64	Pietro Tardonico
864–81	Orso I Particiaco
881–7	Giovanni II Particiaco
887	Pietro I Candiano
888–912	Pietro Tribuno
912–32	Orso II Particiaco
932–9	Pietro II Candiano
939–42	Pietro Particiaco
942–59	Pietro III Candiano

959–76	Pietro IV Candiano
976–8	Pietro I Orseolo
979–91	Tribuno Memmo
991–1008	Pietro II Orseolo
1008–26	Orso Orseolo
1026–32	Pietro Centranico
1032–43	Domenico Flabanico
1043–71	Domenico Contarini
1071–84	Domenico Selvo
1084–96	Vitale Falier
1096–1102	Vitale I Michiel
1102–18	Ordelafo Falier
1118–30	Domenico Michiel
1130–48	Pietro Polani
1148–56	Domenico Morosini
1156–72	Vitale II Michiel
1172–8	Sebastiano Ziani
1178–92	Orio Mastropiero
1192–1205	Enrico Dandolo
1205–29	Pietro Ziani
1229–49	Giacomo Tiepolo
1249–53	Marin Morosin
1253–68	Ranier Zeno
1268–75	Lorenzo Tiepolo
1275–80	Jacopo Contarini
1280–89	Giovanni Dandolo
1289–1311	Pietro Gradenigo
1311–12	Marino Zorzi
1312–28	Giovanni Soranzo
1329–39	Francesco Dandolo
1339–42	Bartolomeo Gradenigo

1343–54	Andrea Dandolo
1354–5	Marin Falier
1355–6	Giovanni Gradenigo
1356–61	Giovanni Dolfin
1361–5	Lorenzo Celsi
1365–8	Marco Corner
1368–82	Andrea Contarini
1382	Michele Morosini
1382–1400	Antonio Venier
1400–1413	Michele Steno
1414–23	Tommaso Mocenigo
1423–57	Francesco Foscari
1457–62	Pasquale Malipero
1462–71	Cristoforo Moro
1471–3	Nicolò Tron
1473–4	Nicolò Marcello
1474–6	Pietro Mocenigo
1476–8	Andrea Vendramin
1478–85	Giovanni Mocenigo
1485–6	Marco Barbarigo
1486–1501	Agostino Barbarigo
1501–21	Leonardo Loredan
1521–3	Antonio Grimani
1523–38	Andrea Gritti
1539–45	Pietro Lando
1545–53	Francesco Dona
1553–4	Marcantonio Trevisan
1554–6	Francesco Venier
1556–9	Lorenzo Priuli
1559–67	Girolamo Priuli
1567–70	Pietro Loredan

1570–77	Alvise Mocenigo I
1577–8	Sebastiano Venier
1578–85	Nicolò da Ponte
1585–95	Pasquale Cicogna
1595–1605	Marino Grimani
1606–12	Leonardo Dona
1612–15	Marcantonio Memmo
1615–18	Giovanni Bembo
1618	Nicolò Dona
1618–23	Antonio Priuli
1623–4	Francesco Contarini
1625–9	Giovanni I Corner
1631–46	Francesco Erizzo
1646–55	Francesco Molin
1655–6	Carlo Contarini
1656	Francesco Corner
1656–8	Bertucci Valier
1658–9	Giovanni Pesaro
1659–75	Domenico Contarini
1675–6	Nicolò Sagredo
1676–84	Alvise Contarini
1684–8	Marcantonio Giusinian
1688–94	Francesco Morosini
1694–1700	Silvestro Valier
1700–1709	Alvise II Mocenigo
1709–22	Giovanni II Corner
1722–32	Alvise III Mocenigo
1732–5	Carlo Ruzzini
1735–41	Alvise Pisani
1741–52	Pietro Grimani
1752–62	Francesco Loredan

1762–3	Marco Foscarini
1763–78	Alvise IV Mocenigo
1779–89	Paolo Renier
1789–97	Lodovico Manin

APPENDIX 2

....

VISITING THE PIAZZA

Throughout the period of the Republic, the main entrance to the Piazza was from the lagoon. Those arriving here by gondola could reach the Piazzetta from the landing stages that lined the southern edge of the square and the quayside along the Molo. This was not only the route used by the doge on important ceremonial occasions, but was also the principal access point for many other Venetians, as can be see from the paintings of Canaletto and other eighteenth-century artists. Some distant sense of this experience of gaining the Piazza by stealth can still be had by approaching it either by ruinously expensive private water launch or by taking the Alilaguna water taxi from Marco Polo airport. It is a slow business (allow an hour), since there are stops at both the island of Murano and the Lido, but the magic of seeing the city rise slowly above the horizon never fails. Those unable to reach the Piazza in this way will percolate into the square from under the arcades that line it, or struggle along the Riva degli Schiavoni with many fellow travellers, or along the equally overcrowded route that runs from behind the Basilica over the bridge beside the Seminary and then into the Piazzetta dei Leoncini. Alternatively, a number of vaporetto stops are within short walking distance of the square.

Both the Piazza and the Piazzetta have been maintained as monumental social spaces, much as the Austrians conceived them in the first half of the nineteenth century, rather than as the more chaotic multifunctional arenas that they were under the Republic. Food stalls, souvenir sellers and the rest are banished to beyond 100 metres of the square itself, and can be found gathered like birds of prey along the Riva degli Schiavoni and behind the Basilica. Corn-vendors, who at one time were the only exception to this rule, have also now been exiled as part of an attempt to reduce the pigeon population (the corn was for the birds, not human beings). Despite its grandeur, the Piazza has been largely abandoned by the Venetians, except for those who work in the square (no one actually lives there), and the sense of intimacy that led the French writer Honoré de Balzac (1799–1850) to describe it as 'a stock exchange, a theatre foyer, a reading room, a club, and a confessional' has largely evaporated. The *listòn* (the Venetian equivalent of the *passeggiata*) has moved elsewhere, and the shops under the arcades selling expensive jewellery and Murano glass cater for well-heeled tourists rather than locals. So too do the Quadri and Florian cafés, whose (unamplified) chamber ensembles entertain with an unchanging diet of Strauss waltzes and arrangements of Frank Sinatra songs throughout most of the year. (It is one of the ironies of life in the twenty-first-century Piazza that many of its 'traditional' musical characteristics are imported from elsewhere – Vienna, Hollywood, Naples.) The most economic (and perfectly affordable) way to see the engaging 1720s interiors of the Florian, whose illustrious patrons have included Casanova, Byron, Goethe and Henry James, is not to take a table in the rooms looking on to the Piazza, but to retreat to the bar at the back.

It is a fact that the vast majority of the millions of tourists who visit Venice every year do so simply to be in the Piazza and nowhere else. So much so that the spectacle of the square crowded to overflowing at midday in the summer months has become something of a tourist attraction in its own right. Even if the population has changed, with visitors vastly out-numbering Venetians, the rituals of participation reconfirm the age-old function of the Piazza as the focus of sociability.

Two suggestions before setting out. Firstly, buy and read a reliable guidebook to take with you. Once inside the Piazza and its museums there is only an extremely limited selection of guides available; they are neither cheap nor very authorita-tive. Labelling of individual objects is often poor, presumably to encourage recourse to the audioguides. Second, book as much as possible in advance in order to avoid queuing for lengthy periods. This can be done very easily via the official website of the city museums at *www.museiciviciveneziani.it* (in Italian, English and French); using one of the commer-cial on-line booking websites is considerably more expensive. The combined ticket (currently 12 Euros) secures admission to the Museo Correr, the Museo Archaeologico, the Palazzo Ducale and the Libreria Sansoviniana. (The more expensive museum pass adds extra museums, some of them in Murano, and is only suitable for those with plenty of time in the city.)

According to the most recent estimates, the most popular site in the complex of buildings around the Piazza is the Basil-ica, which is visited by well over 1 million people every year. It is open daily. Entrance is by the main west door and is free. During the summer months the wait can be long, perhaps as much as 1–2 hours, and it has been known for the queue to stretch the whole length of the Piazza as far back as the Ala

Napoleonica. It is possible to beat the queues, however, by arriving with luggage which then has to be deposited (free) in the deconsecrated church of San Basso in the Piazzetta dei Leoncini; the receipt can be used (whether officially or not is unclear) to go to the front of the queue. Alternatively, bookings can be made on-line at *www.basilicasanmarco.it*. Not all of the building is accessible; the exquisite Cappella Zen, the crypt and the baptistery (with a font by Jacopo Sansovino) are normally kept locked, and can only be seen by arrangement with the office of the *proto* (the architect in charge of the Piazza and its buildings), which is located inside the Basilica. However, it is well worth the effort.

Separate tickets have to be bought to see the Pala d'Oro, placed behind the High Altar, the Treasury (which contains a dazzling display of Byzantine liturgical and ritual objects in silver and gold decorated with precious stones), and the Loggia and Museo della Basilica. Located on the west front above the main door, the Loggia provides an unforgettable vista of the Piazza, while the museum contains the original four horses of Constantinople removed from the façade in 1977. Now safely installed inside a museum and replaced outside by modern copies, these once proud imperial beasts serve as the ultimate symbols of a Venice now completely divested of all political significance, but universally regarded as 'the world's most touristed city'.

On entering the Basilica many feel a sense of disappointment. The interior is dark and in places slightly shabby, and the measures taken by the authorities to order the constant flow of people through the building (some areas are roped off) and to protect the fabric (the astroturf carpeting is particularly dispiriting) impair proper appreciation of the grandeur of the whole. Even more importantly, the mosaics (particularly those of the five domes), which are the great glory of the building, can only be seen when illuminated. At the moment this is between 11.30 a.m. and 12.30 p.m. on weekdays, and more or less continuously, to coincide with the times of Mass, at the weekends. Although the glorious sounds of Monteverdi and the Gabrielis rarely resonate here any longer, sung Mass takes place at 10.30 a.m. on Sundays; there is no need to either queue or book in advance, and entrance is through the Porta dei Fiori in the Piazzetta dei Leoncini. Sunday Vespers involves a procession during which the Byzantine icon of the Madonna Nicopeia, another piece of booty from Constantinople, is displayed. The entrance to the Campanile is through Sansovino's Loggetta. It was from the top (reached by lift; there is a charge) that Galileo Galilei (1564–1642) famously demonstrated the workings of his telescope to Doge Leonardo Donà in 1609. From here the view of the city and of the lagoon is sensational; on a clear day the Dolomites north of the city of Belluno can be seen in the distance.

The most popular of the four museums in the Piazza, with, like the Basilica, over 1 million visitors a year according to the last official figures, is the Palazzo Ducale. Here the queues for entrance through the Porta del Frumento, in the centre of the main façade overlooking the lagoon, are also long, and it is often advantageous to buy the combined ticket to visit all four at the Museo Correr in the square rather than at the Palazzo Ducale itself. In addition to the rich interiors, whose walls and ceilings are lined with historical and allegorical canvases by Titian, Tintoretto (notably the vast *Paradise* in the Sala del Maggior Consiglio) and Veronese, among others, it is also possible to take a guided tour of the lesser-known areas. These *itinerari secreti* (currently starting at 9.55 a.m., 10.45 a.m. and 11.35 a.m.; extra charge) take in the area of the law courts and the offices of the judiciary of the Republic, including the evocative torture chamber (with four cells for prisoners waiting for attention), and the Piombi ('leads'), so-called because of their location on the top floor of the palace directly under the roof. Casanova's cell, from which he escaped in 1756 (the incident is described in his *Storia della mia fuga dalle prigioni della Repubblica* of 1788, translated into English as *Story of My Flight from the Prisons of the Venetian Republic*), can be seen. This frequently reprinted account of the escapade earnt the author as much contemporary fame as did his sexual adventures. The star attraction of the Museo dell'Opera, which is on the ground floor, is the display of the original capitals and columns from the portico of the building. Originally carved in 1340–55 but subsequently restored, they were replaced by copies in 1876–87. From here access can be gained to the central courtyard of the palace, which contains the Arco Foscari and the Scala dei Giganti at the top of which the doge was crowned. The Porta della Carta is best viewed from the Piazzetta.

The Museo Correr contains the collections left to the city by the Venetian nobleman Teodoro Correr (1750–1830), which were installed here in 1922. The entrance is from the right of the portico leading out of the Piazza under the Ala Napoleonica. Some of the rooms on the first floor retain their neoclassical decorations from the Napoleonic occupation; those in the throne room, which include frescoes by Carlo Bevilacqua (1775–1849) and sculptures by Antonio Canova (1757–1822), are particularly fine. The historical collections on display include paintings of state ceremonies some of which took place in the Piazza, portraits of some of the doges (including Francesco Foscari), and the complete set of woodcuts which make up Matteo Pagan's *Procession in St Mark's Square*. Among the works exhibited in the picture gallery is an impression of Jacopo de' Barbari's celebrated map of Venice together with the six original woodblocks that produced it. The collection is particularly rich in works by Giovanni Bellini and his brother Gentile, and is perhaps best known for Vittore Carpaccio's *Two Venetian Ladies* of *c.* 1495; for long thought to represent two courtesans, it is now known to be the lower half of a painting showing hunting and fishing scenes in the lagoon (the upper section is in the J. Paul Getty Museum in California).

In 1593, the impressive collection of Greek and Roman sculptures from the Palazzo Grimani (it was sufficiently renowned for Henry III of France to have visited it on his stay in Venice in 1574) was donated to the Republic. This now forms the core of the collections of the Museo Archaeologico Nazionale, which is entered from within the Museo Correr (usually Room 18 or 19). To be particularly noted are the Grimani Altar (decorated with Bacchic scenes) in Room VI, and the group of three Gallic warriors (Room VIII) found near the Quirinal Hill in Rome. Some of the pieces from the Grimani donation, including the famous Abbondanza Grimani, have now been displayed in the vestibule of the Libreria Sansoviniana in a recreation of the gallery of antique sculpture arranged there by Giovanni Grimani in 1587. The cases in the Libreria contain photocopies of some of the treasures from the library, now subsumed into the collections of the Biblioteca Nazionale Marciana, which is housed in the Zecca in the Piazzetta. The monumental staircase, with a delicate stuccoed vault by Alessandro Vittoria, leads down to the original entrance, and out into the Piazzetta.

SUGGESTIONS FOR
FURTHER READING

On 3 September 1873, John Ruskin wrote to his friend Charles Eliot Norton, the American art historian: 'I am *so* glad you are at work on Venice. You can't have any subject so fine. She's too big for me, now.' If the study of Venice was too big for the extraordinary polymathic intelligence of Ruskin nearly 140 years ago, the size of the literature on every conceivable aspect of the city and its history is now even more daunting. The following is an attempt to reduce it to manageable proportions, while concentrating more on the books that relate to the Piazza San Marco and its history.

In an ideal world, the best place to start would be with Ruskin himself. It would be something of an understatement to describe *The Stones of Venice*, 3 vols. (London, 1851–3) as a guide but, for those with the time to do it, there could be no better way to explore the Piazza than with Ruskin in hand. For those in need of a short cut, try *Ruskin's Venice: The Stones Revisited* (London, 2000, 2nd edn., 2003), a selection of extracts tied to Sarah Quill's exquisite photographs, or the abridged edition edited by J. G. Links (London, 1960; reprinted 2001).

Thereafter the landscape is crowded. For a useful survey

of travel writing about Venice, see John Julius Norwich (ed.), *Venice: A Traveller's Companion* (London, 1990). The best general introduction to the city and its monuments remains Giulio Lorenzetti's *Venice and Its Lagoon*, trans. John Guthrie (Rome, 1961); the Italian original, which first appeared in 1928, has been reprinted many times. Readers of Italian will want to have the conveniently sized Touring Club Italiano guide (currently available in its 1985 edition) in their pockets. One of its twenty-five itineraries is specifically devoted to San Marco. Of the many recent practical guides for visitors to the city, the *Blue Guide to Venice* by Alta Macadam (7th edn., London, 2001) and Hugh Honour, *The Companion Guide to Venice* (London, 1965; 3rd edn., 1990) can both be particularly recommended. Jan Morris's *Venice* (3rd edn., London, 1993), is a classic. Among older guides, almost any early edition of the relevant Murray's Handbook or Baedeker's guide makes fascinating reading and provides a gentle introduction to period attitudes towards the city, while comparisons of different editions betray fascinating shifts in taste, culture, fashion and political attitudes. Beyond purely factual guides there are anthologies which tie specific locations to excerpts from the writings of earlier travellers and writers; two of the most thoughtful are Milton Grundy, *Venice Recorded: A Guide Book and Anthology* (London, 1971, but reprinted many times) and Ian Littlewood, *Venice: A Literary Companion* (London, 1991).

From here it is a short step to historical travelogues, which in practice were often used as guidebooks. Before the age of print these often took the form of private diaries, not intended for general use. However, a handful of these have survived and become invaluable for our knowledge of the Piazza and its life during the middle ages. The sequence begins with the record of the extensive journeys made in three continents by the hildago (knight) and diplomat Pero Tafur, one of the few Spanish travel diaries from the period to have survived. This is available as Malcolm Letts (ed.), *Pero Tafur: Travels and Adventures, 1435–1439* (London, 1926); the account of Pero's time in Venice (also interesting for its misinformation) includes descriptions of the Piazza, the Basilica and the Ducal Palace. Pilgrimage accounts, a distinct medieval genre with its own preoccupations and traditions, are often a particularly valuable source of information about fifteenth- and sixteenth-century Venice; by then the Republic was virtually alone in being able to provide a reasonably secure passage to the Holy Land, and many pilgrims spent a month or so in the city making arrangements for the journey across the Mediterranean, occasionally recording their impressions. Among the most engaging accounts are those of William Wey, written some years after the event, and translated from the original Latin in *The Itineraries of William Wey, Fellow of Eton College. To Jerusalem, AD 1458 and AD 1462; and to Saint James of Compostella, AD 1456* (London, 1857), and more recently by Francis Davey in *William Wey: An English Pilgrim to Compostella in 1456* (London, 2000). A closely observed description of the Piazza and its surrounding buildings, which includes details of works then under construction, is given by the Milanese aristocrat and churchman Pietro Casola; it is edited and translated in Margaret Newett (ed.), *Canon Pietro Casola's Pilgrimage to Jerusalem in the Year 1494* (Manchester, 1907). Accounts of the two pilgrimages to the Holy Land made by the German Dominican Felix Fabri are published in full in Aubrey Stewart (ed.), *The Book of the Wanderings of Felix Fabri (Circa 1480–1483 AD)*, 2 vols. (London, 1896); the second journey contains his description of the Corpus Christi procession, as does that of Richard Guylforde, which can be read in H. Ellis (ed.), *The Pylgrymage of Sir Richard Gwylforde to the Holy Land, AD 1506* (London, 1851).

English visitors to Italy became more numerous in the seventeenth century, with the comparative liberalisation of official attitudes towards travel to Catholic Europe. One of the most lively if eccentric portrayals of the city, including the Piazza, to be found anywhere is to be found in Thomas Coryate's *Coryat's Crudities. Hastily gobbled up in five moneths travells etc.*, 2 vols. (London, 1611), which is more easily found in the reprinted edition, 3 vols. (London, 1776) and in a two-volume edition published in Glasgow in 1905. Coryate is often credited with having invented the Grand Tour, that formative experience which became *de rigueur* for young British aristocrats during the eighteenth century; the phenomenon itself is discussed and analysed, via a wealth of literary sources, in Bruce Redford, *Venice and the Grand Tour* (New Haven and London, 1996). Many followed in Coryate's immediate wake, and a number of them published descriptions of the city and its buildings; for an overview, see John Stoye, *English Travellers Abroad, 1604–1667: Their Influence in English Society and Politics* (2nd edn., New Haven and London, 1989). Among unpublished writings of the period there are many interesting observations in the letters of the poet and diplomat Sir Henry Wotton, who served as English ambassador to the Republic for some twenty years during the reign of James I, and in the diary of John Evelyn, who visited Venice in 1645. For the first, see Logan Pearsall Smith, *The Life and Letters of Sir Henry Wotton*, 2 vols. (Oxford, 1907), and for the second *The Diary and Correspondence of John Evelyn*, William Bray, ed., 4 vols. (London, 1850).

Charming anecdotal glimpses of life in the Piazza during the eighteenth century occur throughout *Venise au temps de Casanova* (Paris, 1969) by Maurice Andrieux, translated into English by Mary Fitton as *Daily Life in Venice in the Time of Casanova* (London, 1972). Appropriately enough, Casanova was the only great Venetian writer of the final decades of the Republic. The Piazza (and famously the prison and the roof of the Doge's Palace) occasionally feature in his lengthy autobiographical account (*Histoire de ma vie*) of apparently endless vigorous street sex; it is available unabridged as *The Memoirs of Jacques Casanova de Seingalt*, Arthur Machen, trans., 6 vols. (London, 1958–60).

Goethe's impressions of the city, formed during his trip to the Italian peninsula in 1786–8, are best approached through the translation of the *Italienische Reise* (published as *Italian Journey 1786–1788* by W. H. Auden and E. Mayer (Harmondsworth, 1970)). By this date the game was almost up, and some prescient sense of the romantic square that was to occupy the nineteenth-century literary and pictorial imagination is already present in Hester Lynch Piozzi [Mrs Thrale]'s *Observations and Reflections Made in the Course of a Journey through France, Italy, and Germany* (London, 1789).

With the end of the Republic in 1797, Venice, now curiously marooned from the mainstream of European political and diplomatic concerns, became a central site for reflection and meditation, and poetic expression in the widest sense. This is most obviously seen in painting and literature. J. M. W. Turner made three trips to Venice; the first in 1819 when he was already forty-four years old, the second in 1833 and the last in 1840, when he was in his sixties. His many depictions of the city and the Piazza critically influenced the development of the notion of Venice as the city of dreams; many of the most important are in the Tate Gallery in London (see Ian Warrell, *Turner and Venice* (London, 2003), published to accompany a major exhibition of Turner's Venetian scenes).

Lord Byron's lengthy narrative poem in four cantos, *Childe Harold's Pilgrimage* (published 1812–18) famously contains, in the influential fourth canto, his sentiments on viewing the prisons from the Ponte della Paglia. (They also fascinated Charles Dickens who visited Venice in 1844 and wrote a characteristically grim description of them.) Alongside the prosaic guidebooks now produced in some numbers, writers and poets turned to the city as never before in its history as a source of inspiration – although not all of them, let alone the audiences for which they were writing, had actually been there. As the protaganist of Robert Browning's poem *A Toccata of Galuppi's* (1842) remarks to the eponymous composer, everyone is familiar with Venice, whether they have visited it or not, through its highly developed image. Browning no doubt had in mind such influences as: William Shakespeare's *The Merchant of Venice* (1596–8) and *Othello* (*c.* 1603), in both of which the doge plays a significant role; Thomas Otway's immensely popular *Venice Preserv'd* (1682); and Ben Jonson's *Volpone* (1605). To these the later visitor might have added the charming period observations of the American consul in Venice from 1861 to 1865, William Dean Howells, in his *Venetian Life* (1866), and in some of the many books by the prolific Englishman Horatio Brown, such as *Life on the Lagoons* (1884), *Venice. An Historical Sketch* (1895), *In and Around Venice* (1905) and *Studies in Venetian History* (1907). Brown, who lived most of his life in Venice (for four years in the fabled Palazzo Dario on the

Grand Canal), was befriended by Ruskin, who admired his scholarship and industry; one of the most intriguing of the nineteenth-century Anglo-American Venetianists, he was a serious antiquarian historian whose major work, the *Calendar of State Papers Venetian* (transcripts of Venetian documents relating to English affairs), remained unfinished at his death.

By this time the novelist Henry James had made his first three trips to Venice, two for short periods in 1869 and 1872, and a more extended stay in 1881, when he stayed at what is now the Pensione Wildner on the Riva degli Schiavoni. Venetian elements are present in *The Wings of the Dove* (1902) and *The Princess Casamassima* (1886), and above all in *The Aspern Papers* (1888), which contains a celebrated description of the Piazza seen from a table in the Caffè Florian. There is also a lengthy section on Venice in *Italian Hours* (1909). Together with James McNeill Whistler (1834–1903) and John Singer Sargent (1856–1925), James is one of a trio of near-contemporary major figures born in the United States who spent major portions of their lives in Europe and became fascinated by Venice. Whistler (who visited the city more than ten times in forty years) included the Piazza among his Venetian engravings made during an extended visit in 1879–80, and also made the Basilica the subject of the spectacular *Nocturne Blue and Gold* (National Gallery of Wales). Sargent painted the Piazza, particularly the Piazzetta, many times – often from the lagoon. For further discussion, see Alastair Grieve, *Whistler's Venice* (New Haven and London, 2000), Margaret F. MacDonald, *Palaces in the Night: Whistler in Venice* (Berkeley and Los Angeles, 2001) and Warren Adelson and Richard Ormond, *Sargent's Venice* (New Haven and London, 2006). The authoritative corpus of Sargent's Venetian paintings is described and illustrated in the sixth volume of the *Complete Paintings of John Singer Sargent: Venetian Figures and Landscapes 1898–1913* (New Haven and London, 2009).

From here the attention moves to Claude Monet, who stayed and painted in Venice in 1908. The *Doge's Palace* completed four years later and now in the Kunsthaus, Zurich, is the best-known outcome; Monet's impressions of the square, which he regularly visited to capture the effects of the morning light, can be gathered from the letters published in Philippe Piguet, *Monet et Venise* (Paris, 1986). This particular tradition more or less ends with the often dark and melancholic paintings of the Piazza and the Piazzetta by the English painter Walter Sickert (1860–1942), who somehow managed to import the drab colours of the Camden School group into his vision of Venice. From there the image of Venice and the square as the embodiment of the city of enchantment passes into the hands of photographers.

Among the other highpoints of twentieth-century literature in the English language that reflect the Piazza and its environs must be counted Ezra Pound's *Cantos* (1915–62). Pound was in and out of Venice for much of his life; his experiences and impressions inform cantos XXIV–XXVI (originally published in *A Draft of XVI Cantos* (Paris, 1924/5)), while the poem 'Piazza San Marco' was published in the *San Trovaso Notebook* (1908). Thomas Mann's novella *Der Tod in Venedig* (1912), translated into English by Kenneth Burke as *Death in Venice and Other Stories* (London, 1925 and frequently reprinted) is, despite its title, actually set on the Lido except for one brief episode in the Piazza (see below). Perhaps the most insistent and concentrated treatment of Venice (including aspects of the Piazza and its surroundings) as the ultimate site of imagination and memory is to be found in Marcel Proust's *Albertine disparue*, the sixth part of *A la recherche du temps perdu* (*Remembrance of Things Past*), left unfinished at the author's death in 1922. The authoritative version of the text of the 'Venetian episode' is a matter of dispute; see Peter Collier, *Venice and Proust* (Cambridge, 1989).

In some sort of way impossible to quantify, all these historians, travellers, poets, writers and artists have contributed to my personal impression of the Piazza, its architectural history, its development and function as an urban and social space and its critical role as a lever of the poetic imagination; this has been assembled over the course of many visits, some long periods of living in the city, and much reading and listening. A number of more specialised (and in some cases technical) texts have also been drawn upon in the course of writing this book. At the level of primary sources, the eyewitness accounts of travellers and visitors mentioned above have been supplemented by other documents from archives (particularly the Archivio di Stato in Venice) and elsewhere. Some are given in English translation in David Chambers and Brian Pullan (eds.), *Venice: A Documentary History* (Oxford, 2001). An authoritative visual survey of the city in maps, a number of which have been specifically drawn upon (and illustrated) here, is presented in Jürgen Schulz, *The Printed Plans and Panoramic Views of Venice, 1486–1797* (Venice, 1970); see also G. Cassini, *Piante e vedute prospetiche di Venezia (1479–1855)* (Venice, 1982), with many facsimile reproductions. Jacopo de' Barbari's magisterial aerial view of Venice, which took three years to construct and then print from six woodblocks, has been reproduced by Giuseppe Mazzariol and Teresio Pignatti as *La pianta propettica di Venezia del 1500* (Venice, 1963).

Of the many general histories of Venice, a necessarily brief selection of works restricted to English might include: George Bull, *Venice the Most Triumphant City* (London, 1980); David Chambers, *The Imperial Age of Venice, 1380–1580* (London, 1970); Christopher Hibbert, *Venice: The Biography of a City* (London, 1988); Frederic C. Lane, *Venice: A Maritime Republic* (London, 1973); William H. McNeill, *Venice: The Hinge of Europe, 1081–1797* (Chicago, 1974); and John Julius Norwich, *Venice: The Rise to Empire* (London, 1977) and *Venice: The Greatness and the Fall* (London, 1981), which can be found usefully combined as *A History of Venice* (Harmondsworth, 1982). Chambers and Norwich for preference if there isn't much room in the luggage.

For the general history of Venetian architecture, three works in particular have been constant companions and invaluable reference sources: Ennio Concina, *A History of Venetian Architecture*, trans. J. Landry (Cambridge, 1998); Richard Goy, *Venice: The City and Its Architecture* (London, 1997); and Deborah Howard, *The Architectural History of Venice* (rev. edn., New Haven and London, 2002). This last is an enlarged edition of a book originally published in 1980, now greatly enhanced by new photographs. In the case of the history of Venetian painting, which enters into the history of the Piazza from time to time if only tangentially, the literature is dominated by monographs on individual artists; the best overall survey is John Steer, *A Concise History of Venetian Painting* (London, 1970). There is no equivalent for music; for the Renaissance period, see Iain Fenlon, 'Venice: Theatre of the World' in Iain Fenlon (ed.), *The Renaissance from the 1470s to the End of the Sixteenth Century* (London, 1989), which lays particular emphasis upon the music in the Basilica and in the Piazza.

In addition to these general works, each individual chapter of the book has drawn upon more specialised works. The more important are as follows:

CHAPTER 1: MYTHS AND ORIGINS

Edward Muir, *Civic Ritual in Renaissance Venice* (Princeton, 1981) is the classic treatment of Venetian civic myths and their celebration in the Renaissance. Patrick J. Geary, *Furta Sacra: Thefts of Relics in the Central Middle Ages* (2nd rev. edn., Princeton, 1990) is particularly useful for the events surrounding the *translatio*. Iain Fenlon, *The Ceremonial City: History, Memory and Myth in Renaissance Venice* (New Haven and London, 2008) places the accent upon the use of music, liturgy and the printing press in the forging of a sense of Venetian identity.

CHAPTER 2: IMPERIAL VISIONS

Eduardo Arslan, *Gothic Architecture in Venice*, trans. Anne Engel (London, 1971) is still useful for the Palazzo Ducale. See also Patricia Fortini Brown, *Venetian Narrative Painting in the Age of Carpaccio* (New Haven and London, 1988), particularly for discussion of Gentile Bellini's *Procession*, probably the most discussed and reproduced image of the Piazza. The scholarly contributions of the Austrian historian and Byzantinist Otto Demus are in a class of their own; his *The Church of San Marco in Venice: History, Architecture, Sculpture* (Washington, DC, 1960) remains the standard work on the Basilica. See also his *The Mosaics of San Marco in Venice*, 2 vols. in 4 (Chicago, 1984). Ettore Vio (ed.), *St Mark's: The Art and Architecture of Church and State in Venice* (New York and London, 2007) is a useful collection of essays on different aspects of the Basilica and its monuments. Deborah Howard, *Venice and the East: The Impact of the Islamic World on Venetian Architecture, 1100–1500* (New Haven and London, 2000) investigates the general phenomenon of Islamic influences and has much to say about the Piazza, while Michael Jacoff, *The Horses of San Marco and the Quadriga of the Lord* (Princeton, 1993) is essential, if controversial, reading on the subject of the four horses. Information about the more important objects in the Treasury of the Basilica is conveniently gathered together in the exhibition catalogue *The Treasury of San Marco* (Milan, 1984).

CHAPTER 3: THE NEW ROME

Norbert Huse and Wolfgang Wolters, *The Art of Renaissance Venice: Architecture, Sculpture and Painting*, trans. E. Jephcott (Chicago, 1990), is a valuable synthetic account with good illustrations, while both Ralph Lieberman, *Renaissance Architecture in Venice 1450–1540* (London, 1982) and John McAndrew, *Venetian Architecture of the Early Renaissance* (Boston, 1980) are standard treatments which contain discussions of the Renaissance remodelling of the Piazza. Manuela Morresi's *Piazza San Marco: Istituzioni, poteri e architettura a Venezia nel primo Cinquecento* (Milan, 1998) contains much new documentation and is essential reading about Sansovino's architectural work in the square, as is the relevant section of the same author's *Jacopo Sansovino* (Milan, 2000) and Deborah Howard's fundamental study *Jacopo Sansovino: Architecture and Patronage in Renaissance Venice* (New Haven and

London, 1975). Bruce Boucher, *The Sculpture of Jacopo Sansovino*, 2 vols. (New Haven and London, 1991), has been consulted in connection with Sansovino's sculptural work both inside the Basilica and on the façade of the Loggetta. David Rosand, *Myths of Venice: The Figuration of a State* (Chapel Hill and London, 2001) deals with the elaboration of the Myth of Venice through sculpture, and particularly painting, in the early period.

CHAPTERS 4: RITUAL FORMS AND 5: URBAN NOISE

For state rituals and processions, see Muir, *Civic Ritual* and Fenlon, *The Ceremonial City*. The material in chapter 5, which attempts to bring the Piazza back to life through evocation of its changing soundscape through time, draws upon many different sources and is essentially the result of fresh research.

CHAPTER 6: DECADENCE AND DECLINE

The eighteenth century is conventionally treated as a period of decadence and decline in Venice, but this stereotype cannot be extended to all aspects of its social and cultural life. For an overview of painting in the period, see Michael Levey, *Painting in Eighteenth-Century Venice* (London, 1959; 3rd edn., 1994); also Jane Martineau and Andrew Robison (eds.), *The Glory of Venice: Art in the Eighteenth Century* (New Haven and London, 1994). All of the major painters (Canaletto, Francesco Guardi, Michele Marieschi) of urban topographical views, many of them made for milords doing the Grand Tour, painted the Piazza many times. For Canaletto, the most accomplished of the group, whose paintings (notwithstanding the intervention of artistic licence) must be considered as important records of life in the Piazza, indeed of its appearance before subsequent changes, see J. G. Links, *Canaletto* (Oxford, 1982) and the same author's *Canaletto: The Complete Paintings* (London, 1981), both standard works.

CHAPTER 7: FROM SPRITZ TO PINK FLOYD

The period as a whole is the subject of a major monograph by Margaret Plant, *Venice. Fragile City 1797–1997* (New Haven and London, 2002). Paul Ginsborg, *Daniele Manin and the Venetian Revolution of 1848–49* (Cambridge, 1979) remains the classic account of Manin's revolt against the Austrians, which was proclaimed in the Piazza. Giandomenico Romanelli *et al.*, *Venezia Quarantotto. Episodi, luoghi e protaganosti di una rivoluzione 1848–49* (Milan, 1998), the catalogue of an exhibition at the Museo Correr dealing with these events, is rich in visual sources. Many of the paintings and engravings illustrated there used to be on show in the Museo Nazionale del Risorgimento in Venice, but this is now defunct and everything is in store until further notice. Literary reactions to the Piazza (Browning, Wordsworth, Ruskin, Proust, etc.) are best approached through John Pemble, *Venice Rediscovered* (Oxford, 1995), and particularly Tony Tanner's occasionally wayward but endlessly insightful and provocative study *Venice Desired* (Oxford, 1992). For Ruskin in the square, see also Robert Hewison, *Ruskin and Venice* (London, 1978). Ruskin's interest in the architecture of the Piazza runs throughout his writings, which can be consulted in their entirety in E. T. Cook and Alexander Wedderburn (eds.), *Works of John Ruskin*, 39 vols. (London, 1903–12).

Films featuring the Piazza are not rare – even James Bond managed to get there in *Moonraker* (1979). But for sheer visual beauty, few can trump Luciano Visconti's version of Thomas Mann's *Death in Venice* (1971), which includes a fleeting glimpse of the Piazza, as does the original, at the moment when Aschenbach (Dirk Bogarde) learns for the first time that cholera has arrived in the city. The Piazza figures more centrally in David Lean's beautifully shot *Summer Madness* (UK, 1955; released as *Summertime* in the USA), in which a middle-aged and presumably virginal secretary from Akron, Ohio (Katharine Hepburn) arrives in Venice from Paris on the Orient Express to begin a three-week holiday of a lifetime. On her first day she goes to the Piazza where she encounters and falls in love with a middle-aged antique dealer (Rossano Brazzi), who turns out to be both married and separated; the meeting (and the square) is central to the story. Ian Softley's 1997 version of Henry James's novel *The Wings of the Dove*, with Helena Bonham-Carter's award-winning appearance as Kate Croy, also includes some spectacular shots of the Piazza in a film which, somewhat surprisingly, rises above the usual limitations of the novel-into-period genre of the Merchant-Ivory school. Away from such things, clips of the legendary Pink Floyd 1989 concert can be explored on YouTube, while longer DVD accounts, both official and otherwise, are available via the web. On this occasion the band played from a pontoon moored in the lagoon, while a huge crowd gathered in the Piazza itself. Almost twenty years later, on 9 July 2008, Sir Elton John played a two-hour concert on a temporary stage placed against the backdrop of the Ala Napoleonica before a somewhat more modest audience of some 4,500 fans. For an entertaining analysis of the present-day attraction of the Piazza as a tourist destination, see Robert C. Davis and Garry R. Martin, *Venice, The Tourist Maze. A Cultural Critique of the World's Most Touristed City* (Berkeley, Los Angeles and London, 2004), chapter 3, 'The Heart of the Matter'. The authors' conclusions tend to confirm Mary MacCarthy's observation that 'the tourist Venice is Venice'. That may be so for the 14 million people who visit the city each year but for the 65,000 Venetians who actually live there the reality is both frustrating and schizophrenic. In the modern Piazza, as in the city itself, two parallel versions of Venice co-exist, often in harmony but sometimes in tension. The drawing-room of Europe has become once again the theatre of the world.

ACKNOWLEDGEMENTS

Many friends and colleagues have contributed to the final shape and tone of this book. Among them I should like to thank in particular Vicky Avery, Pete de Bolla, Simon Goldhill, Deborah Howard, Frank Kermode and Clive Wilmer in Cambridge, and Annalisa Bristot, Giorgio Bussetto, Giulio Cattin, Giovanni Morelli and Mario Piana in Venice. Also to be thanked for their support along the way are Gian Mario Cao, Giuliano di Bacco, Francesco Facchin, Richard Goldthwaite, Allen Grieco, Sara Mathews Grieco, Andrew Hopkins and Marco Spallenzani. The series editor, Mary Beard, has been wonderfully helpful in all sorts of ways. At Profile Books Peter Carson has never faltered in his encouragement, and I have benefited greatly from of the expert eye of Penny Daniel in preparing the text for publication. Sally Holloway who copy-edited the manuscript with enthusiasm and patience, improved it considerably. Much of the book was written in Málaga, some of it in the incomparably peaceful surroundings of the Castillo de Santa Catalina. Many years ago, I went to Venice for the first time with Lewis Lockwood; it changed everything.

LIST OF ILLUSTRATIONS

Osvaldo Böhm, Venice: 2, 3, 4, 6, 9, 16; Cameraphoto Arte, Venice: 1; Iain Fenlon, Cambridge: 7, 10, 11, 14, 25, 28, 30; Inga Groote, Berlin: 24; King's College Library, Cambridge: 18; Kunsthistorisches Institut, Florence: 23, 29; Geoff Moggridge, Cambridge: 22; Museo Civico Correr, Venice: 5, 8, 12, 13, 15, 17, 19, 20, 21, 26; Soprintendza per i Beni Architettonici e per il Paesaggio e per il Patrimonio Storico, Artistico ed Etnoantropologico di Venerzia e la Laguna, Venice: 27.

While every effort has been made to contact copyright holders of illustrations, the author and publishers would be grateful for information about any illustrations where they have been unable to trace them, and would be glad to make amendments in further editions.

INDEX

Figures in italics indicate
captions

[211]

WONDERS OF THE WORLD

This is a series of small books that will focus on some of the world's most famous sites or monuments. Their names will be familiar to almost everyone: they have achieved iconic stature and are loaded with a fair amount of mythological baggage. These monuments have been the subject of many books over the centuries, but our aim, through the skill and stature of the writers, is to get something much more enlightening, stimulating, even controversial, than straightforward histories or guides. The series is under the general editorship of Mary Beard. Other titles in the series are: